LifeLaunch

A Passionate Guide to the Rest of Your Life

Phase I:
"Go For It"

Phase II:
"The Doldrums"

Phase III:
"Cocooning"

Phase IV:
"Getting Ready"

Pamela D. McLean and Frederic M. Hudson

Contributions by Michael McLean Hudson

Table of Contents

Section I: Prepare to Journey Ahead

Chapter 1

Chapter 2

Chapter 3

Section II:
Design your Blueprint, Follow These Maps

Chapter 4

Section III: Launching a New Chapter

Chapter 9

Section IV: Resources for a LifeLaunch

About the Authors

Pamela D McLean, CEO and co-founder of The Hudson Institute of Santa Barbara, *a learning organization focused on transition and change, coaching education, and coaching services*, is an educator, writer and lecturer.

McLean holds a Ph.D. in Clinical Psychology from the Fielding Graduate University and brings 30 years of experience as a licensed clinical and organizational psychologist, executive coach and leader in the field of coaching. She is a speaker on topics of Transitions, Coaching Excellence, and Women in Leadership. Her work is fueled by her passionate interest in how we develop and change as adults at work and at home. Her original research examined how women plan their lives, studying the lives of 500 women and analyzing the significance of intentionality at various stages in life's journey.

She has been on the faculty of Antioch University and currently serves on the Harvard Women's Leadership Board, JFK School of Public Policy; she is a member of Women Presidents Organization, serves on the board of her regional Planned Parenthood affiliate, the editorial board of the International Journal for Coaching in Organizations, Advisory Council member for Women's Center for Applied Leadership, a member of the American Psychological Association, Division 13 of APA in Consulting Psychology, and a Fellow of The American Group Psychotherapy Association.

Frederic M. Hudson co-founder, is a retired educator, writer and recognized expert in the field of adult development. He is widely respected for his contributions to the fields of adult development, career transition planning, human and organizational development, and coaching.

As a Rockefeller and Danforth Fellow, Hudson earned his doctorate at Columbia University in New York and taught at Colby College and the University of San Francisco before moving to Santa Barbara in the early 1970's where he was the founding president of The Fielding Graduate Institute from 1974-1986. In 1987 he and McLean founded The Hudson Institute of Santa Barbara, an international learning organization focused on transition, change and renewal, coaching education and leadership coaching. The central theme of the organization is to teach adults to become masters of change in their lives at work and at home.

Preface

My husband, Frederic Hudson, and I wrote the first edition of this book more than ten years ago. In our original edition we wrote about life as we'd known it growing up and the implications that held for our lives as adults, and we shared some of our experiences in the parenting chapter. Today we have grown children spanning the early-to-late twenties – a rich time and powerful learning for all of us. The early phases of adulthood look vastly different than a few decades ago and we are struck by how much there is to learn from those younger than us!

In our own lives many things have changed. In our original writing, Frederic shared his early life-changing experience with polio (see appendix) and all the challenges that came with overcoming the disease as well as its aftermath and the stigmas associated with polio at that time. Today, as we leave behind the first decade of the 21st century, we've been on a new journey and find ourselves encountering all the challenges, opportunities, and surprises we inevitably confront as we move forward with our lives.

I'm now in my mid-fifties enjoying this step of the journey, the joys of parenting adult children, the satisfaction of the accomplishments on the work front that come from years of passion, work, and commitment to the field of adult development, learning and change. Along the way we've stumbled into one of life's challenges – a chronic disease in the form of Alzheimer's. Frederic was diagnosed with this form of dementia in 2000 and over the past several years we've learned more than we could imagine about living with a chronic disease, especially – one that is shrouded in mystery, fear and mythology.

We've learned that there is life after such a diagnosis and that there are ways to normalize routines and lifestyle to maximize the joy of life in the disease's early stages. For the most part we've accomplished just that. We've met a mighty challenge – the kind we talk about in this book, a variation of one sort or another that we are all likely to encounter along life's path. *But more importantly, we've learned first hand that it's not the crisis or event that's important, it's how we learn to live with it, to manage it, and to carry on and find meaning in spite of the challenges.*

With these experiences in our minds and hearts, it was clearly time to make some important additions and updates to our original work. Much has changed in the past decade, impacting the way our lives unfold. When we wrote our earlier editions our culture was collectively 'enjoying' some of the 'old' stability and predictability about how life unfolds, and we put a heavier emphasis on some points that we no longer believe to be as well suited for our times.

Since then the potential for, and the likelihood of, rapid, dramatic and disorienting change has become manifest, and our new work reflects that. We've taken a closer look at the complexities of the adult journey - the ones that aren't as conveniently organized into the decades of our lives as they once were. Whether it's the first career, the advent of parenthood, marriage, the deconstruction of retirement, our need to react positively to changes forced on us by an increasingly fast-paced and turbulant work, or the vastness of our choices in life today, the landscape has changed forever and our choices and options are more plentiful and endlessly complex. Never have we needed a model for understanding, responding to, and shaping change in our lives like we do today.

We started helping adults navigate the rivers of change thirty years ago. In those days there was an abundance of literature on childhood and adolescent development but very little on the rest of the life cycle. We wanted to give people a map, help them figure out where they wanted to go, help them set off in the right direction and guide them as far as we could. Since then we have worked with thousands of individuals, companies and organizations from all around the world. We've written, researched, and worked with leaders, professionals and talented human beings managing and effecting change for themselves at important turning points along life's journey.

This book offers the reader our experiences, our best thinking and a blueprint for maximizing opportunities that exist up for us during life's changes and transitions if we are open to the possibilities. Our well-known change model provides a practical framework for understanding the natural cycle of change and renewal in our lives, for crafting our life chapters and transitions from the inside out in a purposeful way that lays the groundwork for leading a passionate life.

Throughout this book you'll notice that we use the term 'LifeLaunch' to denote a major turning point in one's life. **We see a LifeLaunch as the beginning of a new chapter of your life. Each LifeLaunch requires fresh vision, new plans, and inner courage as you shift gears from yesterday's commitments to tomorrow's possibilities.**

Because of the ever-changing global world of the 21st century, you will probably have many more chapters in your life than your parents had. Many of us today will enjoy an added 'bonus round' of twenty-some years of life compared to past generations. If you are going to prosper in your elder years, the work starts now! Each of your chapters will likely be shorter than theirs, but you will have more opportunities than they did to change your career, geographic locations, and adult roles.

To thrive in today's world, you need to know how to LifeLaunch whenever the outside world forces change upon you or your inner self demands it – whether age 25 or 65!

Acknowledgements

This book reflects the encouragement, reflections and contributions of so many – it is truly a team effort that brought this new edition to the finish line!

First, to all who have participated in our LifeLaunch programs over the past twenty-five years – we thank you for your insights and we continually learn from your experiences in working with our models and materials.

Second, we are most grateful to many colleagues who read through parts or all of the manuscript along the way. Your feedback, recommendations and perspectives were enormously valuable to us and provided a tremendous sense of support along the writing journey. A very special thanks to the very thorough writing eye and skill of Barbara D'Amico! Great thanks to Kim Woodward for his important contributions to reflective practices we can apply to all transitions. Great appreciation to Tom Pollack, Lynn Schoener, Bill Lindberg, and Toni McLean for your careful reviews. An equally important thank you to the members of the Hudson Leadership Team who have been at the helm of this program for many years now. Your insights, experiences and innovations have added to our understanding of the transition process.

Third, a most appreciative thank you to Linda Antone at the Hudson Institute headquarters, who combed through each version of this manuscript adding her careful edits and wisdom and oversaw the entire project from beginning to end.

Our middle son, Michael, was enormously helpful in providing his perspective on the FirstLaunch transition and all of the complexities of the twenties.

Finally, with gratitude to our partnership, as we crafted the original work on our model of transition and change, and continue to hone and refine the concepts.

Foreword

How You Will Benefit From This Book

Life changes come in many forms – there are the big changes that tend to catch us off guard – we aren't looking for them, we are never ready for them; some are exhilarating while others are far less than welcome. Perhaps it's a major promotion, a mid-life marriage, a job loss, a divorce, or an unwanted move. And then, there are some big changes that simmer just under the surface for long periods of time until we are ready to awaken the possibility of a shift or transition in our life from a place deep within ourselves – it may be a career position we've been thinking about leaving, a marriage we know is no longer alive, a persona we want to relinquish.

May you live all the days of your life.

— Jonathon Swift

We can't easily predict how the beginning of a new chapter of our life might come about. Rarely do we hear stories about someone making a big change in their life because a plan *simply came to them in the night* and led them to craft a new chapter. Instead we may contemplate a big change for several years or be jolted into a change with few options. Whether it slowly steeps or is thrust upon us, transition and change is part of the predictable landscape in our adult journey.

It's our experience in working with hundreds of very talented and resourceful people over the last twenty years that most of us spend more time reacting to changes that surprise us, than we do in the listening to our own inner stirrings and yearnings so that we might craft intentional new chapters/transitions at the inevitable crossroads in our adult journey.

Blueprints for Change

Whether we like to admit it or not, most of us aren't in the habit of inviting change into our lives or actively seeking opportunities for big changes. As humans, we seem naturally drawn to what is comfortable and known in the familiar routines and demands of our lives. Ironically enough, what seems to be most predictable is that we tend to be surprised and caught off guard when change comes our way. We see it as it happens to others, we read about it, we know life itself doesn't last forever; and yet, we are almost always taken aback by change when it is at our doorstep.

> *It is not the strongest of the species that survives, nor the most intelligent, but the one most responsive to change.*
>
> — Charles Darwin

Change might come in the form of an opportunity for a new career move in a different location; an organizational downsizing that spells lay-offs; a death in the family; a shift from college years into the adult journey; a chronic disease to manage; a decision to take an early retirement; a divorce, or any other number of possibilities. No matter how change comes your way, **this book creates a blueprint that allows you to nurture your resilience in responding to those surprising changes and to foster an environment in which your inner urges for change are alowed to flourish.**

Our "blueprint" for managing change is reflected in our 'maps' which catalog and symbolize the essential elements of the "whole person". We've developed a foundational map for understanding and optimizing the ongoing cycle of change – our Cycle of Renewal, and we've created a series of additional 'maps' that represent the primary aspects of the whole person in the mosaic of life.

We begin with a map that examines the ongoing Cycle of Renewal and we add to this the essential dimensions of purpose and values, roles and systems, the adult journey, the work of learning and unlearning, and the overall vision that supports our plan. These maps help us track the new data on our wants and needs critical to charting a new course.

LifeLaunch is the beginning of a new chapter of your life. Each LifeLaunch requires fresh vision, new plans, and inner courage as you shift gears from yesterday's commitments to tomorrow's possibilities.

What's Changing? What's Not?

Each LifeLaunch is a graduation from one era of your life into the next. Society used to tailor our LifeLaunches for us, and guide us down established paths of adult life. No more. Today you must design your own path, and take charge of all of your LifeLaunches no matter what your age or situation.

Marker Events

We have any number of 'marker' events in our adult journey that create some decision points, some forks in the road for us to contend with – either passively or with a proactive engaged approach. Well-known 'markers' include leaving home, completing college, getting married or finding a life partner, buying a home, figuring out the first career steps, and making a choice about having children.

In the earliest part of our adult journey we have few anchors in place to guide us, we are called upon to engage in some intentional crafting of our lives: the first job or a career path is a familiar guidepost. Maybe we choose a city or location where we've got family or friends, and use this as the anchor for launching; per chance we transform a part-time college job into something full-time for a bit; or perhaps we summon the courage and the sense of purpose required to take a bigger leap and create a new chapter that is uniquely suited to a deeper calling.

Stories are our nearest and dearest way of understanding our lives and finding our way onward.

— Ursula Le Guin

In the years from post-college to mid-life, the pace quickens and we often find ourselves locked into responsibilities, roles and commitments that render us less likely to be spontaneous. We become tightly tethered to roles, expectations and life's realities. As the years press on, the stakes grow higher on all fronts and trade-offs become tougher to negotiate. Intentional change requires a vision for the future combined with plenty of courage and planning.

In the past, we have tackled all of these decision points without wasting much time (and too often with little reflection) because we had a much more predictable roadmap about how to proceed. Today, our wiser youth are mulling these big turning points for much longer periods of time, feeling more in control of the choices and more interested in following their own path rather than a traditional, prescribed route. This new way of managing life's big choices means that we need more tools for effective transitions – tools for making decisions, for managing change and for gaining clarity about what matters most at any given point in our lives – tools like the maps laid out in the chapters that follow.

Your past cannot be changed, but you can change tomorrow by your actions today.

— David McNally

Typically, the first major transition time occurs for most of us in our twenties as we leave home or college to assume full responsibility for our lives. The only other adult transition time celebrated by the entire culture is what we've long termed 'retirement'. In between, most of us make several transitions, without many maps and blueprints to guide us. This book provides you with some blueprints for change in the form of maps and models we developed for guiding yourself successfully through all the adult territory. You will learn how to design and plan, proactively, for several new transitions between your twenties and your retirement, and in your later years as well.

With more than half of our nation now beyond the 'young adult years,' mastery of midlife and elderhood has more urgency and importance than ever before. This book will help you plan all of your years with new skills and confidence. You will identify the best paths for your journey into challenging life/career choices. If you apply to your life the six maps contained in this book, you will evolve clear life plans for successful LifeLaunches for the rest of your life – from the springtime of young adulthood to the autumn years of elderhood.

You need a set of tools to shape, execute, and monitor each of your LifeLaunches. These tools are in this book, along with explicit directions on how to use them.

• Each LifeLaunch integrates the themes of work, love, family, leisure, and social commitments in new ways as you move into your future.

• You will understand how 'change' can work to your advantage – at work, at home, and in your personal life.

• You will tap your passion for living your best choices for the years ahead.

Suggestions

• Use this book as you would a personal journal. Read it slowly, a little bit at a time. Meditate on the themes that speak to you. The salient concepts are deliberately restated throughout the book so you won't lose sight of the essential ideas. Interact with what you read. Write your own thoughts in a companion notebook or journal that you create as you read this book. A paper trail of your ideas is the best medium for constructing an inspired plan for your future.

- Before you begin each chapter of the book, look at the outline provided in the Table of Contents which will help you get an overview of what is being presented. The Index will also help you find items in the book useful for your LifeLaunch.

- In each chapter concentrate first on understanding the ideas being presented. Then apply them to your life through the questions and exercises provided for your personal reflection and application. Read each question as if it has your name on it. If it engages you and fits your needs, work it through in your notebook, in writing, so you can keep track of your thoughts. If any item does not speak to you, read on.

- If you are married or living with a partner, consider reading the book together so you both can talk about how you want the next few years to be. A committed 'couple' is often the best unit for planning the future during the adult years, validating your 'separate' as well as your 'together' plans.

- Talk with close friends about your findings as you read along so you get feedback, validation and encouragement as you evolve a plan. If you have a number of friends wanting to construct new life plans, set up a study group that meets every couple of weeks, taking a chapter at a time. This book is an excellent tool for group discussion and discovery – at home, work, or church.

- Stay with the book to the very end because the ideas you discover – chapter by chapter – will guide you systematically to your emerging plans and next LifeLaunch.

It doesn't happen all at once...you become. It takes a long time.

— Margery Williams

Section One

Prepare to Journey Ahead

Chapter One

What is the Future
You Want?

It takes a lot of courage to release the familiar and seemingly secure, to embrace the new. But there is no real security in what is no longer meaningful. There is more security in the adventurous and exciting, for in the movement there is life, and in change there is power. — Alan Cohen

What is the Future You Want?

Making It Happen

The future doesn't drop into our laps – prefabricated – the way it used to when society programmed the traditional path for just about everyone. In today's chaotic swirl, you get the future you want by making it happen.

We call it 'entrepreneuring the future,' taking responsibility for your life direction as fully as you can within a world of constant surprises. The world we face is a dizzy flow of shifting options, so in order to shape your preferred future you need to know what you really want, and then get to work.

'If you don't know where you're going, any road will get you there', acording to Lewis Carroll, and the push-pulls of life around you will shape your path – to somewhere you haven't chosen but have to adjust to. You can do better! Choose your destinations carefully, set your sails, find your crew, use your compass, and venture forth to make your best future happen.

If you want a future with your name on it, then dream your dream, construct your plan, and make 'you' happen. Your ability to sort out what belongs on your path from what doesn't is perhaps the most important ability you have.

Even if you have explicit goals and objectives, you have to keep reevaluating them and adapting them as situations around you change. The good news is that you have more paths to consider than ever before. The bad news is that you have less predictability about where your decisions will lead you. Our world today has more possibilities and less surety for everyone on earth in making choices. That's the way it will be for the twenty-first century – more choices along with less control and reduced predictability.

As life proceeds over years, much stays the same, but more changes – a blending of many sources, a process never fully finished, a flow of beginnings and endings. You are all the time coming together and falling apart, holding on and letting go – in several dimensions and directions of your life, simultaneously and continuously.

The daily pressures to act, to do, to decide, make it difficult to stop and think, to consider, and to examine your life goals, directions, and priorities – to find the best choices you have for managing your own world.

— Roy Menninger

Adults are living about twenty-five years longer than adults at the beginning of the twentieth century. Those twenty-five extra years come at the end of your life, so if you are going to be potent, awake, and happy in your old age, you need to know how – at your present age – to develop your talents through the years ahead. Few of us know how – at our present age – to develop our emerging strengths through the years ahead. Few of us know how to grow older with increased lucidity and expectancy. This book is an effort to unleash that knowledge.

The secret to a resilient life in our kind of world is in knowing how to invent yourself, over and over, letting go of what is no longer you, taking on new strengths, and shaping new chapters for your life, guided by your own emerging vision. 'What we're seeking is an experience of being alive,' declared Joseph Campbell, 'so that we actually feel the rapture of being alive.'

You are the only one who can open the doors into the next chapter of your life. After all, it's your LifeLaunch. Use this book carefully and deliberately, to link your life to your vital dreams and possibilities. Keep a pen and notebook handy as you read, and write out your own thoughts, concerns, and priorities whenever they occur to you.

Backing into the Future

You probably burst into your post-adolescent years with great excitement, but felt unprepared for the long haul ahead. When we trade in our early years for older ones, we enter alien adult territory. We all grow older feeling terrorized by the mirror, surer of how our bodies are changing than how our lives are progressing. We know who we are, but we have to imagine and believe who we're becoming. That takes vision, trust and courage.

Even in our thirties or forties we may feel that the gates are closing on what's possible rather than opening up to the rest of our lives. We all revel in the joys of youth, but few are expectant with the joys of getting older, even if all the 'older' means is that you're not as young as you were. Few of our early dreams extend very far into our mature years, and when they run out, our expectancy usually shrinks and shrivels. All too many of us run out of dreams long before we die.

Only through intense personal effort do you learn that every closing gate is also the beginning of a new adventure you are never fully prepared to take. You always have opportunities for blending each ending into a new beginning if you have imagination and skills for writing new script for your life – to begin a new life chapter. Shifting gears from chapter to chapter in your life is a critical life skill, particularly if you want to seize your optimal choices for the years ahead.

The secret to every LifeLaunch is looking ahead, to be visionary with the time and space in front of you as you get older and more experienced at life. All you have is time, so measure your life deliberately and learn from it constantly. Refuse to be trapped or limited by your past and your youth. Your past is a launching pad, not a fence; a school, not a prison. Your future begins with what you do today to make tomorrow happen – to dream and be courageous with your life so you can become 'more.' Learn how to lean into the wind.

The people who get on in this world are the people who get up and look for the circumstances they want, and, if they can't find them, make them.

— George Bernard Shaw

The key is to put your energy into anticipating life rather than into fixing the problems of your past. The single most important ingredient to a successful life is to remain proactive – to concentrate upon prospective, vital, enchanting options – and mapping your way into 'tomorrow' with deliberate decisions, risk taking, realism, and caution.

Being an adult is an evolving thing, and most adults are amazingly uninformed about their own potential throughout the long haul of grown-up living. That is why this book on LifeLaunching is so important. This book describes the contours of adult life and how you can chart your journey ahead with both confidence and concrete plans.

The Tightrope of the Working Mom

When you're immersed in a family and career, it's virtually impossible to plan your own life. "How can I ever find time, day to day, for my future?" is a familiar refrain of working moms who consider devising a more intentional plan.

There is no denying that a 'plan' for a working mom is a far different proposition than the development of a plan for a working father or a working woman without children. One major difference is **sheer time**.

Not so many years ago I was balancing it all – a working mom, with three children in their growing up years, entrepreneuring my career while moving headlong into midlife. I often became frustrated when I pondered the next chapter of my life, because my life was so intertwined in the lives of others. Yet I wanted desperately to be clear about my life and to chart my way ahead, even as I was caught up in a wonderful and never-ending three-ring circus all around me.

I've come to believe that a clear purpose is even more important in the midst of the continual demands and maintenance that is a natural part of balancing the family and work tightrope. I needed to be clear about a mission in my life that transcended housework, school lunches, after school activities, and bedtimes – in order to invest well in those important and constant duties.

Plans for women, in particular, who are balancing the tightrope of work and family must be flexible, yet definite; short-term, yet possible. Working moms must not stop living, dreaming, and designing their own lives. Even though much must be postponed, something should always be in the planning basket, ready to hatch. Without that we lose our zeal for life, our vitality, our compassion for ourselves.

Refrain of a Mid-Fifties Woman

Today, I'm at one of those junctures in life where I seem to easily fit into many of the stereotypes and crisis points we all read and write about in the field of transition and change. I'm in my mid-fifties, I'm entering what Bernice Neugarten long ago termed the dreaded 'empty nest'. I'm looking in the mirror and seeing a reflection of someone that doesn't quite fit the image I have etched in my mind and in old photos. I'm fully engaged in a career I thoroughly enjoy and I'm feeling more passionate, focused and on purpose than ever. Yet, I'm well aware that the 'clock is ticking' and that creates a whole new level of intentionality to all I do. I'm mindful that time might not be on my side and I want to savor all that is important and tackle all that is on my list of aspirations for the future. And, in life's natural unfolding of unanticipated circumstances, I'm one of thousands who joined the ranks of 'caregiver' several years ago when my husband was diagnosed with early onset Alzheimer's.

My story doesn't seem much different than most of my fifty-something compatriots. I notice a convergence of passion, a sense of newness and possibilities, and a powerful intention to craft some compelling chapters ahead. And once again, we are at the frontier of change. No surprise that we aren't drawn to the models for fifty- and sixty- something women in the past. We've got tons of work and life experience, a longer life path ahead, a history of passion and pension for change. We've all read the newspaper and magazine articles touting the fifties as the new forties, the sixties as the new fifties – you get the idea. Truth is, there is more fact than fiction in this for those of us who have spent our adult lives combining the passions of our work with the profound and important work of raising responsible children capable of taking on the challenges of tomorrow.

For me, the days of balancing work and family seem largely in the past, and while much about those days is now a blur in my mind, one thing I am certain of is that maintaining a sense of purpose while balancing endless priorities was an important challenge I held onto throughout good times and the wild ones as well. Like many, I knew from a very early age that I wanted to make a difference in the world, I wanted to make a contribution worthy of something, and I wanted to have a fulfilling family life. Those of us in our fifties can now chuckle together about the unrealistic sense of possibilities we had on this front and bravo for us. There are still many doors to open for women, but we turned the latch, we started the conversation, we built some bridges, we created awareness, and we did it because we possessed a passion that is still very much alive.

What's ahead for me – I'm thoroughly energized by my work, my writing, and my teaching, and there's much more to accomplish on all fronts. I'm committed to making a difference on some important issues in our world and I'm walking my talk through investing time and expertise on causes I believe in. I'm enjoying this new stage in my family and savoring the

Change and growth take place when a person has risked and dared to become involved, experimenting with his own life.

— Herbert Otto

ways we can come together and support one another in the adult journey. I'm more appreciative of the friends in my life than ever before and consciously nurturing those relationships. I'm noticing a stronger and stronger call to make more time for reflection, alone, in nature, for periods of time. And as a caregiver who clearly has a long road yet to travel, I'm devoted to finding ways to be a "giver of care" for my husband of thirty years that are loving and tender, while leaving space to pursue my dreams and passions along the way.

The rest of this chapter is devoted to stories of adults who have struggled with changes in their lives. The stories of Jim, Gloria, Charlie, and Martha are addressed to you, to share their experience of a LifeLaunch. The descriptions of Jim and Gloria are brief vignettes of adults who have not adapted creatively to change. Charlie and Martha are examples of persons who learned and grew as they worked through the turning points of their lives.

> *If you don't know where you are going, any road will get you there.*
>
> — Lewis Carroll

Jim

Jim, an executive in his fifties, is not very different from the way he was in his twenties. He works hard, makes good money, and invests carefully. He's always busy looking for more, more, more of what he's always wanted. That's his life, his script, and his story.

Even though he has mastered the challenges of the first forest he entered as a young man, he hasn't journeyed further to find the clearings deeper in the woods. He still lives and dreams as if he were twenty-five – rushing about, solving problems, and organizing the world around his entry-level priorities and skills.

Over the years, he hasn't internalized the advantages of his age and experience. He hasn't asked new questions or explored the emerging currents of his own life. He hasn't challenged his ego or laughed at his narcissism. He hasn't knocked on the doors of his imagination to explore who he truly could become, in midlife and beyond.

Two months ago Jim was 'let go' by his company. Even though his benefit package was more than fair, Jim never saw it coming and was absolutely undone. His work had been his life. His past was all he knew. How could he start all over? Within days he was depressed and at the beginning of a profound transition which would prepare him for the rest of his life.

Gloria

Gloria, who married early and devoted her life to raising three children hasn't known what to do with herself since her children left home. She feels abandoned by her familiar world and out of sync with the career world of her new female friends. Rather than use her past as a resource for her future, she feels contained and limited by who she used to be.

She wants to find fulfillment but can only focus on what she perceives she doesn't have and bemoans that her only developed talent is caretaking. Gloria also feels trapped by the limits of her previous roles and is caught up in her own negative agenda about her current situation. She doesn't know how to translate her experience into a new LifeLaunch and break out into the world of money, careers, and unabashed leadership. She feels 'less' because she has not explored 'more'.

Charlie and Martha

Charlie and Martha seemed to have it made. Everyone thought Charlie was successful. At age 44, he had a good salary, a managerial position, a new marriage with a step-family blend of four kids, a fairly nice house in the suburbs. In his fifth year at a computer firm, he was respected and admired. He thought of himself as successful until an economic downturn struck and his firm began to panic and downsize. For sixteen months Charlie worked harder than ever before – around the clock as though he could guarantee his future by how hard he worked in the present.

Then a bell went off in his head: he found himself daydreaming much of the time – evaluating his path and searching for answers to questions he had never asked before about life priorities, family time, his career, and the future. Until then he had devoted his life to just 'doing his best' with whatever was on his platter – particularly his career roles. He had loved challenge and the satisfaction of getting the brass ring, and had always pushed for more and more! Now he wanted a different formula. *"No matter how things turn out at the office, I want my life from now on to be different than in my twenties and thirties. As*

much as I love my work, what I really want is more time for living –
more quality time with things I care deeply about. Somehow I want
to become more 'whole', but how? And how can I make significant
changes without losing what I have already achieved?"

Charlie spent months pondering his deeply held values, his
triumphs and trouble spots, his unused abilities and his latent
dreams. His life review took much longer than he wanted before
he evolved a definite plan that built solidly upon his past yet
gave him a different future.

When he finished evaluating his life, he felt vital again and
was able to negotiate most of the changes he wanted without a
midlife crisis or emotional confusion. He talked it over in depth
with his wife, Martha, his children and friends. This was his
new life plan:

• Charlie decided to start his own small business where he
  could be his own person, instead of being a cog in someone
  else's wheel.

• He created a weekly schedule of home and work commitments
  and planned out his calendar for a whole year, including
  weekly events with the kids and three major trips along with
  Martha. He joined an athletic club and renewed his love for
  tennis.

• He described his new beginning like this: *"I feel like one person*
  again, highly motivated and much more at peace with myself. My
  priorities are clearer than they have been in years, and they come
  from deep within me. Even though I know it won't be easy to keep
  my new life in balance, it's my life. I am – at last – marching to my
  own drum, connected to what I love most, and I am one hundred
  percent committed to the directions I'm now taking. Frankly, that's
  all that matters."

Charlie had designed the scenario he wanted to make happen,
created a plan and timeline, and began a new chapter in his
life. He accepted full responsibility for his choices. He was on
course through conscious dreaming, planning and courageous
actions. He was entrepreneuring his future.

Concurrently, Martha was extraordinarily busy – with family, house, career, friends, and commuting. As a human resources professional at a firm about an hour from her house where she had worked for twelve years, she had her hands full, not to mention her life as wife, mother, and householder.

"Frankly," she confided to her closest friends, *"managing a stepfamily of four kids between the ages of seven and eighteen is my most difficult job. Charlie does his best to help, but he just isn't there most of the time. I've got to be here, and so I work it out. But I feel exhausted, overextended, and out of synch much of the time, Sometimes it seems that all I do is help others live their lives. And that's got to change. But how? And when?"*

As Charlie planned his future, Martha did the same to arrive at some new formula for balancing her life. She loved all the parts but felt they didn't add up to HER. This became her new life plan:

• Martha decided that for the next five years she wanted to be at home more and at work less, even if it meant less money. She saw this as a temporary decision, and she wondered what the impact on her career would be. *"Will I be able to realize my promise and become the leader I always believed I could be?"* she wondered, *"Or will I be more complete if I settle for less?"* For now, at least, her decision was to downshift her schedule, to downsize her commitments, and to upscale her personal agenda.

• Martha rearranged her time at work. That was the really big item. Her boss was surprisingly receptive to her recommendation that she go on a two-day work week in the office and work one other day from her home.

• She also decided to join a reading group to put her in touch with her new friends and ideas.

• She enrolled in a yearlong leadership training program for women to give her an opportunity to evaluate her real leadership abilities and interests, and to provide her with an 'ace' on her resume should she need it if and when she returned full-time to the workforce.

There is nothing like a dream to create the future.

— Victor Hugo

- Martha planned out family trips for a year in advance, hired more help to manage the household, and after a few months on that new schedule she was in charge of her life again. The many parts of her life were more balanced, and for the first time in fifteen years she had the beginning of a private life – which benefited everyone, including Charlie.

- Martha challenged Charlie to see their new directions as something more than moving checkers to different places on the board. *"I want us to be a total team in everything."* She urged, *"So that you know – as I do – which of our children needs to go where to be with whom each day, so you can interchange with me with any of the multitude of tasks that have to get done to make our family and home work. OK?"* And while Charlie said he would do his best, they both knew that he had stretched himself about as far as he knew how – for now – and that his new business was going to be the central event in the new chapter of his life, as it had always been for him.

Overall, however, they both felt they made considerable progress, individually and as a couple. They had evaluated their lives and charted paths that contained both continuities and changes. They believed they had broken the bonds of slavery to everything the world wanted them to be, and were writing their own stories around quality choices – creating their own adventures on their own terms.

Your Turn, Your Journey

Like Charlie and Martha, you can chart your journeys ahead by using this book to plot your future, to make a plan and to be "on course" again. Begin your journey with the questions that follow:

1. List five things you really enjoy doing (cycling, cooking, traveling, jogging, reading, gardening, spending time with friends, renovating houses, etc). This list is a great beginning for getting ready for the future. How can you make these five activities more important in your next chapter?

2.Conduct a career review, assessing your satisfaction and dissatisfaction with your work life and prospects.
Write out your evaluation in this format:

• List what you like and want to keep doing in your job or career.

> *It is not easy to find happiness in ourselves, and it is not possible to find it elsewhere.*
>
> — Agnes Repplier

• List what you don't like and don't want to keep doing in your job or career.

• List how you want your career to look five years from now – personal roles, rewards, and challenges.

3. Choose at least two questions from below that you find very important at this time in your life. Write out your first thoughts.

- How can I move from getting ready to live, to really living?

Is there something in your life you would like to change? If so, first change your perception of the problem. When you can see yourself and your situation differently, you have already taken on the responsibility for your success.

— Marilee Zdenek

- How can I deepen my connections to those I love most, and still be me?

- How can I be at my best as a spouse and parent as my family matures?

- How can I be more caring and sensitive to my parents' needs?

- How can I find work that is a calling, and not merely a source of money?

- How can I find more balance in my life?

Chapter Two

Your Number One Issue: Managing Uncertainty

Go seeker, if you will, throughout the land…. Observe the whole of it, survey it as you might survey a field. It's your oyster–yours to open if you will. Just make yourself at home, refresh yourself, get the feel of things, adjust your sights, and get the scale. Everyone has a chance, regardless of birth, achievement, golden opportunity–to live, to work, to be a self, and to become whatever his or her humanity and vision can combine to make. — Thomas Wolfe

Your Number One Issue: Managing Uncertainty

What's Changing?

My mostly adult children love to hear 'mom's phone story' – it's a funny tale of change, for sure! I grew up in the Midwest in the fifties and sixties and the first ten years of my life on the prairie included a wooden box on the wall of our kitchen complete with an earpiece, a megaphone and a phone number of 'two longs and a short'… at the beginning of the sixties, this system was replaced by a sleek black rotary phone, but still an unusual one – our phone was connected to the same 'party line' as seven other families–undeniably, no place for a romantic teenage rendezvous! Today I barely use my home landline; my trusty iphone downloads my office calendar, emails, instant messages, latest picture albums, acts as my alarm while I'm on the road, and takes photos when my other gear isn't accessible.

> *Change cannot be avoided…Change provides the opportunities for innovation. It gives you the chance to demonstrate your creativity.*
>
> — Keshavan Nair

The velocity of change has increased leaving many over the '40' mark less at ease than their children with technological equipment! Still, change is here to stay and we will experience more and more of it as time marches forward. In the second decade of the 21st century, it's clear we have more chapters in our lives than our parents or grandparents. Each of our chapters seem to be shorter than theirs and the opportunities that exist in relation to our work lives, our shrinking globe, our choices of adult roles and more, continue to grow in complexity and richness. To live with a sense of purpose and satisfaction today, we need to know how to recraft our lives at every step in our journey.

Each chapter is an unfolding and reshaping of you from one era of life into the next. Society used to tailor these chapters for us in a fairly uniform fashion. First, you finish your education, then you get a job, then you find a life partner, settle down, buy a house, have 2.5 children and work toward more and more success until you can afford to sit back and retire.

What's changed about this formula? For better or worse, just about everything. Today, there is less predictability about the move from college to adult life; instead we see a deepening shift in the ways our youth are taking on this passage. More variety, less structure, more travel and volunteer work interspersed with a traditional college education. Less drive to find the 'right' first career move and more interest in an expanded exploration, an entrepreneurial emergence in the decade of the twenties. Demographics tell us that the expectation of 2.5 children is largely a thing of the past. Most married couples and life partners are both working, and the decision to have children (and how many) comes later and has become much more deliberate and thoughtful.

If that's not enough, the notion of retirement is now being turned upside down as we live longer and feel motivated to engage in our world in a vastly different way than past generations. Adults in their 60's and 70's retire, unretire and retire again, looking for ways to stay engaged in the workforce out of either desire or necessity or some combination of the two. With that timeline in mind, it is more important today than ever before that we design our own path and take charge of each of our opportunities no matter what our age or situation. In the past society mostly tailored our adult chapters for us. Those days are gone for good, and if we are willing to take the challenge of crafting our own paths, we take the reins from society by shifting and adapting according to our inner rudders.

The Age of Uncertainty

Have you had an eye exam lately? The optometrist places lens after lens in front of each eye until you say you can see clearly. Think of an era as a bunch of lenses that all the people in a culture look through to see clearly. These lenses provide people with a perception of the world that fits the cultural beliefs of the era. People who share a culture or society perceive the world much the same.

Most developed cultures in the first half of the twentieth century looked at the world through lenses prepared to see evolving stability, progress, and in the U.S., the good old 'American dream". The second half of the twentieth century brought with it the lens of change – the world of technology burst wide open and brought with it immeasurable shifts in industry, technology, communication and more. Family and community life became fragmented, divorce rates climbed, nuclear and extended families were no longer within driving

---

For most people, life is a search for a proper manila envelope in which to get themselves filed.

— Clifton Fadiman

radius, and the pace of work life quickened.

Now, well into the twenty-first century, the sense of change is palpable at work, at home, in our communities and throughout the global community. We are managing the challenges of global warming, shifting demographics, the constant presence of terrorism, the dynamic forces of volatile economies and new world powers.

The lenses that we now see through are change, change, change. People today see the world as challenging, demanding and at times, bewildering and overwhelming. The forces of change seem to have no containment, limits or predictable sources of control. This perception of the world leads us to feel uncertain about our lives and society. And if you are uncertain for very long you begin to believe that the culture you are in is, in fact, declining and becoming dysfunctional. This, in turn, fosters cynicism, fear and hopelessness.

Those of us still wearing the old lenses have increasing difficulty seeing the astounding advantages of the new paradigm – the global marketplace, worldwide civilization, multicultural peoples, new careers, technological advances, transnational political structures and more.

It is not any one nation that is in decline, it is our outmoded beliefs and expectations about stability and progress that are restraining us from seeing the advantages of living in our current environment. It is not too late to help one another see the future as a promise rather than a burden, to see the ready assets of our times instead of the liabilities of our institutions and shrinking world.

In a world of complex change, we need to have skills to 'LifeLaunch' our own lives through the peaks and valleys of our cultural turbulence. Without thoughtful training few of us have the skills to see the opportunity and the "fun" in new.

We are daily buffeted by a random, disruptive flow of the unexpected. We find ourselves reacting to issues and factors we did not realize affect us directly – an increasing unrest in key geographic areas, a growing religious fundamentalism around

Life is not the way it's supposed to be. It's the way it is. The way you cope with it is what makes the difference.

— Virginia Satir

> *The bigger temptation is to settle for too little.*
>
> — Thomas Merton

the world, an aging population that is not reproducing itself in parts of the world (Japan leading the way with Western Europe following), a burgeoning youth population in underdeveloped areas of the globe, and significant economic challenges. In the U.S. we are contending with out-of-control healthcare costs, eroding educational systems, violence of epic proportions and political systems under seige given the challenges they are called on to meet.

It's all too easy to get the impression that the world as we've known it is falling apart. We hear it in all of the 24/7 news that is channeled to us through all forms of media, each seeking its own dramatic spin on already dramatic events. Bad news, hysteria and crises sell, and we become mesmerized by endless global crises we can't do much about. We pipe chaos and tragedy into our living rooms and bedrooms, and then into our brains and nerve endings. The world may be worse than it ever was, but thanks (or no thanks) to technology and the media, more than ever before in history we consume as our central diet shocking stories about violence, misery and human failings from all over the globe.

Yet the same technology brings us amazing new learning tools and programs that nourish the human soul. Let's face it: you have a choice. You don't have to watch thousands of people get killed on television or constantly hearing interpretations of the latest world tragedy over and over and over again. You can be 'informed' and still spend more time actively engaged in meaningful activities like reading, obtaining new skills through learning, or serving some cause you believe in. It all depends on how you see the world and your future in it.

One way leads you to feel less empowered and more passive and helpless. The other way–taking change as the fundamental prism–leads you to feel that the human prospect has expanded and is more accessible to more people, but this requires strong personal monitoring of the limitless number of opportunities and dilemmas presented to us.

The challenge is to find ways to shape your life around the flow of change, the experience of uncertainty and the advantages of dissolving and emerging environments.

We all know, at some level, that the world of the future isn't going to look very much like the world of today. But this doesn't mean our lives and culture are going to be worse off overall. Our future is neither guaranteed decline nor an incline. It's just going to be different. As the population continues to increase and the environmental impact grows we will need to find ways to adapt through transportation alternatives, energy conservation and more. In all likelihood, some aspects of our lives will get better and some will get worse. **However, we will decide, individually and collectively, if the overall impact of change on our lives increases our cynicism and shrinks our expectancy, or deepens our will-to-live and challenges our sense of purpose.**

Do you feel, overall, that you are diminished or extended by the changing environments of your life? How can you get the flow of change in your life and find new promises, horizons, resources and passions throughout all your years? Read on to find out.

Existence is a strange bargain. Life owes us little, we owe it everything. The only true happiness comes from squandering ourselves for a purpose.

— William Cowper

Your Turn, Your Journey
Evaluate Your Prospects

1. What would you say has changed your life for the better, improving your life choices and human prospect during the past ten years? Make a list.

2. What would you say has changed your life for the worse, diminishing your life quality and human prospect during the past ten years? Make another list.

> *The journey is the reward.*
>
> — Taoist saying

3. Whom do you know who seems to thrive on the changes taking place in our lives today? What is he or she like, and what are the specific qualities that make him or her effective in a changing environment? Are these qualities you want to pursue in yourself? What other qualities?

4. How do you think your life will be better and worse five years from now? (Consider career, home life, economic factors, health, etc.)

5. In what ways are you better off and worse off than your parents?

6. Imagine it is the year 2025. What do you think will be much the same, and what will be very different? For example, how do you imagine these things will be: housing, schools, community and family life, career pathways, energy sources, transportation systems, technology, world religions, the shrinking globe, terrorism, global warming and more.

7. What are your ways of managing uncertainty? Think carefully about how you sustain your integrity and dreams when the world swirls around you. Write down, draw or doodle your ideas.

Chapter Three

How To Keep Winning When the Rules Keep Changing

The way we see events approaching us affects the way we respond to them; the way we respond to them affects the way we regard ourselves; and this in turn affects the way we see new events. — W. Timothy Gallwey

How To Keep Winning When The Rules Keep Changing

Two Worlds – Yesterday and Today

Weaving together our growing up years into today's world is a bigger task than ever because the gulf between then and now is growing at such a meteoric pace. In my own life the list is endless: I attended a small rural high school with less than twenty students in my graduating class, while my younger child graduated from a high school class of over 500 students. My family acquired our first television when I was ten years old, while many of today's toddlers are riding in cars with TV screens built in for their viewing enjoyment! I grew up close to a large extended family and lived in the same house until I left for college. Today, our nuclear family is largely scattered around the country and the average stay in a family home is around five years for most of us.

And then, somehow, there are the miraculous convergences we experience when the past and the present seem to magically weave together. About a year or so ago, my grandmother died at the remarkable age of 107. She was cogent, engaged, cooking, embroidering, and staying connected to others through old-fashioned correspondence! I remember when her great grandchildren installed a 'new gadget' into her home – a DVD player...she didn't think she'd ever use it; it was just too complicated and thoroughly unnecessary! A few months later while I was visiting her, a neighbor stopped by to drop off a DVD for my grandmother and as she set it on the counter, she said 'Nellie, you can watch this as many times as you want, it won't even hurt the darn thing, so enjoy it... and by the way, you'll remember the story – it's about The Titanic!'

We Live between Eras

It is becoming more and more difficult to connect the chapters of our lives to one another – from childhood through the adult years, to elderhood. Our adult lives used to be programmed by more or less stable, linear conduits–careers, families, neighborhoods, churches, community organizations–that connected us as individuals to our entire life cycle. Today our lives have increasing amounts of surprises, complexity, and often times cynicism.

> *All real change is grounded in new ways of thinking and perceiving.*
>
> –Peter Senge

For most of the twentieth century, the world we lived in seemed fairly dependable, uniform and evolving – and so our lives took on those dimensions. We were fairly optimistic. Today we are vividly aware that our world is turbulent, unpredictable, and fragile, and our lives are naturally internalizing these qualities. Whether it's the post-modern times, the post 9/11 mood, the global warming challenge, the threats of terrorism, our current economic conditions, or the greed and corruption factors, our lives today may feel more tentative and we are less optimistic and expectant. How could it be otherwise? The central force that shapes our consciousness today is change – coming at us from every direction, like global tidal waves washing away the rocks of the past.

In the last few decades our perception of the world has shifted from a stable, orderly, steady-state model to an unstable, disorderly, change-driven one. Yet most of us live as if the steady-state model were fully operative, or ought to be. We rage or whine when we find it isn't so. Most of us expect to have life plans that will lead us with assurance toward definite security, happiness, and financial prosperity. In the twenty-first century, that's a prescription for misery. Instead, we need to learn how to fulfill our lives within the change process that dominates our lives and our era, rather than view our lives as declining from the promises the generations before us lodged deeply in our psyches. This is a time to change the paradigm, the picture in our minds of how life works best today.

We've clung to four old rules that need to be replaced today with four important new rules. They look like this:

Everything that happens to you is your teacher. The secret is to learn to sit at the feet of your own life and be taught by it.

–Polly B. Berends

The Old Rules	The New Rules
1. The Linear Rule	1. The Circular Rule
2. The Outside-In Rule	2. The Inside-Out Rule
3. The Learning is Just-for-Kids Rule	3. The Learning is Lifelong Rule
4. The Steady-State Rule	4. The Continuous-Change Rule

THE OLD PARADIGM
The Four Old Rules

1. The Linear Rule – This rule promised progress for those who are honest, play by established rules and work hard. According to this old rule, our lives, careers, economy and culture were supposed to keep getting better, year by year, generation by generation–if we simply did our best and followed the culturally prescribed rules. If we veered from this linear pathway we would undoubtedly be viewed as a bit 'off course'. "To be a winner" or "Just do what you're told" was the mentality surrounding the rule rather than today's mantras of "pushing the envelope", "becoming assertive", "being the master of your universe"! This linear rule was the experience of our parents and generations before them and it looked something like this:

Every man dies. Not every man really lives.

–Wiliam Wallace

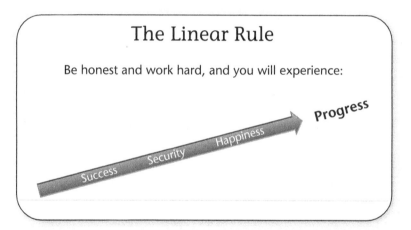

The Linear Rule

Be honest and work hard, and you will experience:

Success Security Happiness Progress

2. The Outside-In Rule – This rule said your personal life is defined and determined by the directives of the society around you. From this point of view, the boxes of life around us shaped and determined our personal choices – communities, families, work systems, the nation and the globe. Nobody talked about "life planning" because people thought their lives were already planned by the world around them.

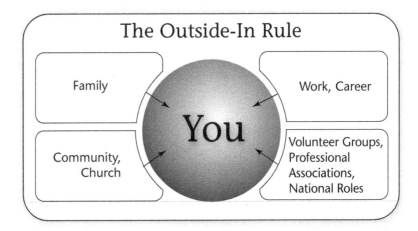

According to this rule, to succeed as a human being, follow the advice of the systems around you: the official authorities in schools, religious organizations, work organizations and governments. The containers of your life will keep you happy, successful, and secure according to the outside-in rule. The external forces are more stable, permanent, and reliant than you are, according to this rule.

3. The Learning-is-for-Kids Rule – In the linear world of the twentieth century, learning was the central business of children and young people, to launch them into stable adult careers, family life and leadership roles. Once launched into the adult years, adults shifted from 'learning' to 'work' as their main activity. Throughout the rest of their years, training outside of work roles played a very minor role.

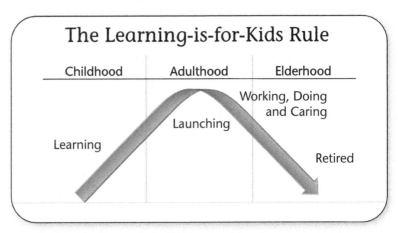

There was no basis for thinking that there were new skills and human competencies needing to be learned and developed throughout the lifecycle. Learning was a central function of young people, not adults – to prepare the way for the initial plunge toward success. Each of us would get molded during our younger years and then hopefully function like personal dynamos the rest of our lives. The notions that adults would need and want to learn continuously and recraft and relaunch themselves several times during the adult journey was thoroughly foreign.

4. The Steady-State [The Great Plateau of Life] Rule – This rule promised that if we worked hard we would each arrive at a steady state or plateau of security for the rest of our lives. Truly, this was the deal, like a cultural reward for falling into line.

There was a long stretch of time when the notion of arriving at a 'steady state' that was largely prescribed to us by the social mores in existence; perhaps you can see this dynamic in your parent's lives. Undoubtedly there was a curious comfort in having a strong sense of how one's adult years would likely unfold. And yet, it often lacked a plan for our most imaginative possibilities.

We are all on a spiral path. No growth takes place in a straight line. There will be setbacks along the way…There will be shadows, but they will be balanced by patches of light… Awareness of the pattern is all you need to sustain you along the way.

— Kristin Zambucka

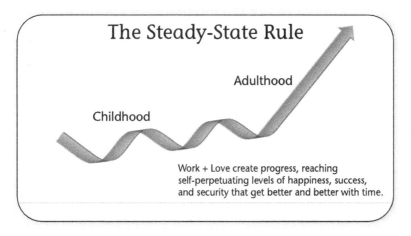

The Steady-State Rule

Childhood

Adulthood

Work + Love create progress, reaching self-perpetuating levels of happiness, success, and security that get better and better with time.

Welcome to The New Rules

Ever so gradually through the final decade or two of the twentieth century, the old rules lost the universal appeal they had held for so long. The old rules required a culture high in continuity, control, and agreed-upon authority, and as those features began eroding during the past few decades, we started to feel that something needed to change in our communities, our governments, and us. The more we strived to live by the old rules, the less thet worked.

Our cultural crisis is our loss of purpose – our confidence, hope, and belief in the future. Many, if not most of us, live lives that are more tentative than expectant, more worried than motivated, more self-absorbed than enchanted, more indulgent than planning ahead. After the lofty adventures of the twentieth century, our entry into the twenty-first century has been dramatic and challenging at home and around the globe. Our balloon has lost its air and we lack the mental maps for traveling confidently into the new territory of our current millennium.

The way ahead requires that we change our expectations, our perceptions, our vision of how life works – and come up with rules and ways of being that empower our lives and institutions in the context of the rapid change that defines our time. Most of all we need to believe in ourselves again–both as individuals and as a people or culture.

If we replace the four old rules with the new rules that are both fair and empowering for our lives in our kind of world today, we can restore confidence, quality living, productivity and leadership with amazing speed and effectiveness.

If we had no winter the spring would not be so pleasant; if we did not sometimes taste of adversity, prosperity would not be so welcome.

— Anne Bradstreet

TODAY'S PARADIGM
The Four New Rules

1. The Circular Rule – Life itself, with its recurring seasons, is a self-renewing process. Our lives today are measured mostly by cycles and chapters, not by linear accomplishments. This rule is the best basic model for empowering your life today.

I still find each day too short for all the thoughts I want to think, all the walks I want to take, all the books I want to read, all the friends I want to see.

— John Burrows

Think of your life as a story, with many chapters. Each chapter itself has a beginning, an end, and a transition to the next chapter. Of course this is sometimes imprecise and often only apparent in retrospect, but there is a certain pattern to life that we've observed in our many years of studying and working with people. Chapters are when our lives "do" something important; transitions are when our lives come apart, veer off track, shift gears, and seek renewal. This is the basic model for understanding your life in today's world. Measure your life in small units of "script' that dramatically describe who you are, with whom, and doing what. When that script loses its passion, becomes tired, outdated, and hard to sustain, you ride the waves of change – called a transition, and either modify your script or come up with a new one. That's the circular rule, as you continuously weave and unravel your life.

Your life is in continuous change, and for the most part it doesn't get better or worse, it gets different, as it forms or reforms chapter after chapter. If you view your life this way, you can feel comfortable in our kind of world, and challenged by change instead of undone by it. That's a maxim for today's life.

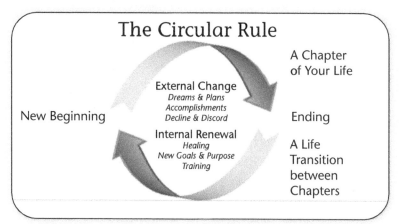

Perhaps this is the most important thing for me to take back from beach-living: simply the memory that each cycle of the tide is valid, each cycle of the wave is valid, each cycle of a relationship is valid.

— Ann Morrow Lindbergh

Applying the circular rule to your life requires high levels of personal confidence, self-responsible behavior, and trust in forces beyond your control. To use this rule, you need to know how to:

• Design the chapters of your life throughout all of your years,

• Become the leader and choreographer of the chapters of your life,

• Embrace necessary transitions between each chapter of your life and invent the main themes and dimensions of your next chapter, and

• Make renewal of yourself and your social context the central features of your life.

The circular rule is about beginnings and endings. It is about an ongoing process of self-renewal, growth and discovery. Typically the cycle begins with a strong inclination to make something important happen and ends when that effort no longer works or seems important. Beginnings are romantic times, fostering passionate commitments. Endings require us to let go of some dream or effort that has gone stale or awry, and either fix it or find a different one.

• Learn how to cooperate with change, to use change as an opportunity for growth and discovery in each chapter of your life.

• Learn how to begin each new chapter of your life with spirited determination to make it succeed – to shape it in the ways that are most meaningful to you.

• When your chapter is thoroughly worn out and exhausted and the end is just a matter of time, design your own exit – begin again, savoring and relinquishing.

• Learn how to reconstruct your life through conscious transitions as you seek new clarity on your choices, your priorities and your purpose.

2. **The Inside-Out Rule** – To stay "on course" in a world that is going in a thousand directions at once, you need to be value-driven and purposive. You need to be anchored in your beliefs.

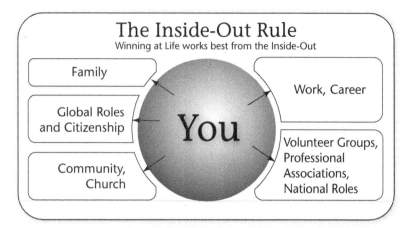

The Inside-Out Rule
Winning at Life works best from the Inside-Out

Family

Global Roles and Citizenship

You

Community, Church

Work, Career

Volunteer Groups, Professional Associations, National Roles

> *In the depth of winter, I finally learned that within myself there lay an invincible summer.*
>
> — Albert Camus

Otherwise, the winds of change will blow you in a different direction with every breeze. To succeed as a human being, you need to be living with purpose, shaping your commitments in the world around your abiding beliefs and concerns. Your many roles as an adult – at work, home, play, community and the rest – are meant to be extensions of your inner self, your core values. Stay anchored to your abiding beliefs and pursue goals you believe in.

Manage your life from the "inside-out," aligning your inner values and beliefs with your broader commitments and roles. Find outer resources to support your fiery purpose. Stay responsible for your destiny, and link up boldly to others in ventures you truly believe in. Become one person with many roles.

Develop a plan for living from the "inside-out" that might include:

• Creating a quiet space in your life for reflection each day, or even once or twice a week. It's almost impossible to stay connected to the central focus of your inner self without cultivating a regular practice of reflection. You might develop a walking ritual, a meditation, a yoga practice or a simple quiet space for self to emerge. This is your time to deepen the inner dialogue and seek clarity about your central purpose at this time in your life.

- Seeking out regular contact with a long term friend who is willing to listen, offer frank feedback, and engage in a dialogue about life today and tomorrow.

- Trying a hand at journaling, jotting down thoughts and ideas. Some recommend this as a regular morning practice; perhaps you will find it useful even once a week to open a door to your inner dialogue that might otherwise remain closed.

- Taking a solo retreat – find a secluded, restful place to journey to once or twice a year, preferably alone. Use this as an unstructured time of renewal, reflection and discovery.

3. **The Learning-Is-Lifelong Rule** – **The key to everyone's future is Learning! It's the way you stay awake throughout your adult years, gaining new interests and tools, stretching the learning possibilities and expanding one's horizon. People who make an unwavering commitment to learning stay fresh and alert. They have new information and powerful ideas. They lead passionate lives, knocking on the doors of tomorrow. More than any other single activity, learning is what separates adults into two categories: the proactive and the reactive (the empowered and the passive).**

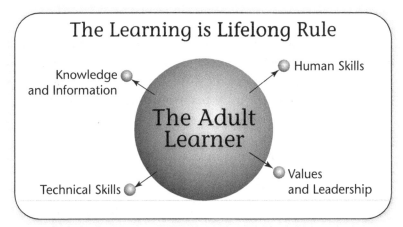

When you "learn," you increase your awareness, concern, and knowledge about something. You disturb your own mental stability to create positive change for growth and discovery. You 'rattle' old beliefs and thinking habits. Learning is the essence of self-renewal, the most positive form of human change. The adult learning agenda has at least four different areas you are apt to have under continuous exploration:

To live a goal-directed life means to have the desire, or even the feeling of obligation to see one's life culminating in certain results... People who live this way always seem to know where they are going and to hold only themselves responsible for their fate.

— Charlotte Buhler

- **Knowledge and Information:** Much of the knowledge you acquire during your younger years is outmoded and must be replaced several times throughout your lifetime. To be awake and effective throughout your years, you have to unlearn what is no longer relevant or accurate and then learn from the creative edge of today's information explosion. At no time has this been truer than today!

  You can always create for yourself a learning program to become significantly better at something by the end of each month, and each year. If you do, you will actually become significantly better at many things, because the act of learning something opens you up to see, hear and become.

- **Human Skills:** You need more than information and knowledge to make the adult years a positive journey. You need to be an effective generalist, competent at any number of skills including speaking, writing, listening, persuading, leading, caring, or managing conflict. What human skills do you need to acquire today to be effective in the settings where you work and live?

- **Technical Skills:** Most of us today require substantial expertise within some specialty career area. We live in a highly technological age which is continually evolving and changing at a breakneck pace. We don't lack opportunities to learn the latest skills; instead we often lack the determination necessary to stay at the cutting edge of our fields and to discipline ourselves to stay on the cutting edge.

- **Values and Leadership:** Adults perform the leadership roles in our societies and we are the bearers of culture from one era to another – through mentoring relationships, voluntary causes, executive and leadership roles, and family ties. As we get older it is natural for our learning to become more and more about values, caring, and becoming generative. If this is a stirring in your life today, chances are you are at least midway along the adult journey.

  What are the learning projects that might prepare you for your leadership roles today and in the future? Write them down and build some of them into your plan for the next chapter of your life.

The only way to make sense out of change is to plunge into it, move with it, and join the dance.

— Alan Watts

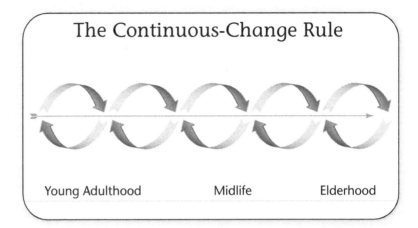

*Every new learning
is life renewal.*

— Frederic Hudson

4. The Continuous Change Rule – Navigating the journey is more important than the destinations, since all arrivals are temporary. There are no static resting places, only continuous change throughout all of the years of our lives. People who perceive their lives as a cycle know there is no arrival at a steady state of crystallized happiness. Process, not progress, becomes the familiar reality.

As you get older you keep revising and renewing the same familiar issues, the same urges, the same concerns you have always had – only you do this in ever changing settings and circumstances.

You chart your way, guide your life, anticipate tomorrow, have your victories and defeats, evaluate as you proceed, change course as necessary, experience losses and gains, and assume responsibility for your destiny.

In our kind of world, competent persons need to know how to renew themselves, over and over – to weave together whenever possible, and to unravel it when necessary. If you do that you will perceive change as a challenge – an opportunity to learn, discover and grow.

If you can commit to what is of lasting worth while learning new directions to explore, you can thrive on change and find a future containing challenge and fulfillment.

Let the new rules provide dependable guides for finding comfort and empowerment in our kind of world. Take your time to internalize them, in your words, in your settings, for

your life. Then move on to the chapters ahead and apply the maps and models to your own life, to see where you want to be and do in the next chapter of your life.

Your Turn, Your Journey
Try It...

1. The Circular Rule of Chapters and Transitions: Imagine you are composing a short autobiography and you begin by constructing the basic outline of your life story to date. Reflect on the past two or three decades (this will, of course, depend upon your age!) and see if you can easily discern the chapters, the times of significant "doing", and the transitions, the times of great change. Go a step further and craft a 'working title' for your autobiography.

Life is a daring adventure or it is nothing.

— Helen Keller

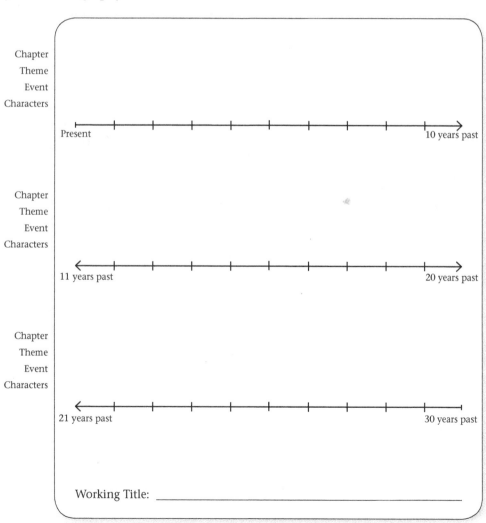

Chapter
Theme
Event
Characters

Present | 10 years past

Chapter
Theme
Event
Characters

11 years past | 20 years past

Chapter
Theme
Event
Characters

21 years past | 30 years past

Working Title: _____

2. The Patterns in Your Life. Now serve as your own literary critic and ask yourself these questions:

- What are the central themes of my life so far (it might be love, career, heroic actions, sports, adventure)?

- What have been my "happiest," most "successful" moments?

- What have been my most "unhappy" times or times of personal failure? Knowing we tend to learn the most from our failures, what learnings stand out for you from any significant failures?

- What were the conditions surrounding my endings and transitions (relationships, loss of dreams, bad luck, health challenges, career moves)?

- What themes and events and persons are essential to the next chapter in my life?

3. How can you sustain an **effective learning agenda** in your current or next chapter; building knowledge, improving your human skills, technical skills, and values and leadership abilities?

- **Knowledge and Information:** Take a quick inventory of your current needs and interests in the area of 'new learning', if you were going to construct your own 'learning program', what might you include in it today:

My Knowledge & Information Learning Program:

Knowledge & Information that would further my career aspirations (a new skill or certification in my specialty area, a new leadership skill, an advanced degree, etc):

-

-

-

> *I have no doubt whatever that most people live in a very restricted circle of their potential being. They make use of a very small portion of their possible consciousness. We all have reservoirs of life to draw upon, of which we do not dream.*
>
> — William James

Knowledge & Information that would positively impact my interpersonal relationships (friends, life partner, children, etc):

-

-

-

Knowledge & Information that would be fun, creative, and adventuresome at this time in life (becoming a pilot, learning a new language, re-reading Shakespeare's works, etc):

-

-

-

A round man cannot be expected to fit in a square hole right away. He must have time to modify his shape.

— Mark Twain

Human Skills: Choose from the following any ideas that might work for you:

- Spend an hour each week browsing your favorite bookstore or library for books and magazine articles that are appealing to you. Pick up something new and different – stretch yourself.

- If you have children at home, create a study group with two or three couples or single parents to discuss parenting issues and strategies for using the home as a learning center.

- At work, try arranging a brown bag lunch once a month and focus on an article relevant to human skills in your industry.

- If you are facing a big transition, join a support group (in person or online) that is focused on the issues you are facing.

- Take an adult education course in some area in which you want to make a contribution or explore a lost hobby.

- Get involved in your church or club in an area of community concern.

I am not bound to win, I am bound to be true. I am not bound to succeed, but I am bound to live up to the light I have.

— Abraham Lincoln

TIPS
To Strengthen an Inside-Out Approach:
Try Out a Reflective Practice

Engage in an experiment for the next thirty days; try out some reliable methods for developing a reflective practice. Here are some options; see if one might work for you:

- Take up **journaling** for the next 30 days. Find a predictable time each day to spend 10 – 15 minutes jotting down your thoughts, ideas, and any associations relative to the day or the recent past. Once every few days take a look for any themes that might be emerging, underline them, track them, see if they lead you somewhere.

- 10,000 **Steps a Day** for the next 30 days. According to cultural anthropologists, this is about the number of steps taken daily by our ancestors. Give it a try; you'll have plenty of time for contemplation while you are getting some great exercise as well!

- A Month of **Yoga or Tai Chi.** Find a studio close to home and sign up for some classes for the next month. Maybe it's a class or two a week and you might try a few different variations to see where your interest is – gentle yoga, stretching, yoga for work, etc.

- A 30-day **meditation practice.** Many of us feel we can't do meditation because we can't sit in lotus pose for an hour with a perfectly quiet mind. Instead, just take 5 or 10 minutes (it's helpful to use a kitchen timer) in a quiet place and sit in an upright chair with your spine straight and your eyes closed, notice your inhalation and exhalation, and notice what your mind does. Afterwards, note what happened in your journal. Experiment with other types of meditation. The book *Meditation For Dummies* by Stephan Bodian has instructions for a variety of meditations.

Section Two

Design Your Blueprint, Follow These Maps

Chapter Four

Maps To Guide You Through Change

To keep alive and effective, you anticipate difficulties and opportunities. You adapt, changing and growing as the individuals and the world around you change, and you periodically recommit yourself to your mission. You act to preserve what is best and discard the rest...Developing a mission means seeing a pattern in the things and thoughts that get you moving; assessing your resources; then formulating your feelings into words. — Charles Garfield

Maps To Guide You Through Change

The Cycles of Our Lives

Life is filled with trade-offs, and while the old rules our parents lived by provided plenty of instructions and prescriptive plans for the adult journey, they often lacked a certain creativity and freedom to carve one's own path. The new rules of today turn those very trade-offs upside down and leave us with more options for building our own unique pathway than we sometimes want! We have more choice, more guaranteed change, more options for 'doing it our way' and less predictability than ever before in history. The trade-offs of today are clear – the landscape is shifting so dramatically that we are able to craft our journey in just the way we choose to; the downside is that endless choices don't generate clarity about what it is we want at any point along the way.

The secret of man's being is not only to live but to have something to live for.

— Dostoyevsky

Change is now the primary reality that shapes and distorts our lives, invading our personal lives at more levels and dimensions than ever before. The constant intrusion of change is both a threat and a resource as our life unfolds. We have spent over twenty years working with individuals managing change, making big and small transitions, and seeking renewal in this often arduous process. Our work, our writing, and our research led us to develop a powerful change model and a series of 'maps' that support a holistic perspective at all points on life's journey. Each of us is far more than a role, a 'twenty-something', a retiree, a student or simply a passionate human being. There are essential facets of the self that we need to incorporate into our being into order to remain self-renewing adults capable of managing the sea of change of today. We offer six maps for understanding the essential elements of the adult journey as you move through life's many chapters.

- **Map 1** will help you stay in charge of your life, whether you are up or down. You will discover how to tap the cycle of change for designing the rest of your life, to use change as a major resource for your future life designs.

- **Map 2** will guide you to seek clarity about your current core values as you shape your next chapter, so you feel alive and purposive. This is where you find your compass for the journey you are about to take.

- **Map 3** will help you prioritize your most important "activities" and "roles" so you connect yourself to your preferred future. This ensures you are living from the inside-out rather than allowing your role to become you.

- **Map 4** will help you explore the predictable changes that take place in adult lives from ages twenty to ninety, suggesting ways to take advantage of whatever your age may be.

- **Map 5** will evoke from you a definite learning agenda, identifying specific skills and abilities you want to master for the journey ahead; and articulating what needs to be "unlearned" in order to move into a new place.

- **Map 6** will provide an integration of your purpose, vision and plan.

Map One
Composing Your Life
Chapters and Transitions

This chapter focuses on Map 1 - our Cycle of Renewal, a compelling model for mastering change in your life and understanding the value of the natural cycles of life as we travel the good times and the difficult ones along the way. You will discover creative ways to plan your life in stable and uncertain times and no matter how change is impacting you; you will learn that there are ways to invest in growth, discovery and new meaning! The Cycle of Renewal model is a powerful tool you can use to master change in your life.

You are Your Story

At the end of the last chapter you constructed an outline of your life story – chapter-by-chapter, event-by-event. In that exercise, you were the author, the main actor, and the literary critic. You are your story as you plan the future as well. You extend certain themes-events-characters, and introduce new ones, as your life rolls on. You write the script and evaluate the story. The more you understand yourself as the story teller and creator of your story, the more you will produce new stories and script for both the next chapter of your life and the transitions between those chapters.

Today, all of our life stories must find comfort and congruence with an increasing volume of discontinuity. You need to know how to find meaning and opportunity in valleys as well as peaks, in transitions as well as the chapters of life.

All of our lives proceed in a never-ending cycle – through chapters of relative stability and shorter periods of relative instability which we term 'transitions'. From birth on, we measure our lives through peaks and valleys, highs and lows, stability and instability – over and over again.

Your life is an autobiography unfolding, a never finished sculpture, a work in progress – with chapters of external achievement and accomplishment followed by periods of internal rearrangement and renewal. The temporary destinations you reach are much less important than your ability to manage and enjoy the journey itself.

In spite of warnings, nothing much happens until the status quo becomes more painful than change.

— L. J. Peter

During most of the twentieth century the relative stability of our society hid this ongoing cycle of change in our lives. Most of us believed that our lives were measured by only one phase in the cycle of change; our external "doing" – and goods. Now, as our world is in such dramatic flux, each person, family, and social unit must learn to navigate through the whitewaters of our time.

Everyday adult life includes good times and bad; up-time and down-time as well; and this is not a personal failure or a decline in cultural history that makes it so. Instead, we simply understand more and more about the patterns of our life paths within our current reality of ongoing change.

The Pattern of All Change

There is a definite pattern to our experience of change just as there is in nature, the ebbs and flows, the seasons, the decay and renewal of plants and cycles of the sun. In life, as in nature, when you know the pattern and where you are in it, you can identify the best choices for guiding yourself, no matter how much change you are enduring.

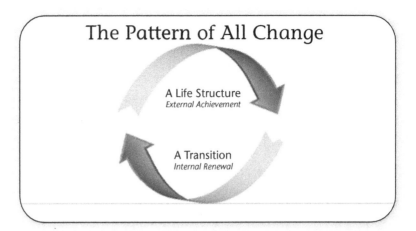

The Pattern of All Change

A Life Structure
External Achievement

A Transition
Internal Renewal

If you are familiar with this cycle, and are comfortable with its flow, change will seem less like a destroyer and more like a conveyer of your life. If you try to contain life to the good times when the sun shines and only good things happen, you will feel diminished and lost when the inevitable thunderstorm begins. You become a change master when you can find meaning and purpose in all the seasons and conditions of your life. The change cycle is a renewal experience for each of us, and the systems of our lives as well.

When you were born, you were most surely in an unfamiliar environment in which you were intensely mystified. In time you learned about a familiar world of sustenance and comfort, of sounds and sights – much of which revolved around your mother and father. By the end of three or four months you had experienced two sets of tools for managing change:

- Stable behaviors – For getting through predictable, structured events, where you are oriented and committed, with familiar routines (sleep time, nursing time, holding and cuddling time).

- Transition behaviors – For getting through unfamiliar, unstructured events, where you are confused and disoriented, with unclear roles (strangers in the midst, unfamiliar noise, shifts in the feeding routine, and new pains of teething and more).

Infants and children go through several stages of development, each of which involves a transition (in which they lack confidence, behave awkwardly, and eventually discover new ways to forge a life direction) and a new period of relative stability (in which they have confidence, pursue goals, and sustain relationships). Children and adolescents experience several cycles of transitions and stable times before they leave home to enter the adult years.

Until recently, we assumed that all this came to a screeching halt when we became full-fledged adults, when we supposedly arrived at steady personalities and behavioral constancy. If we had very many changes in our lives – career shifts, new geographic locations, change of mates, new interests – we were considered unstable. Something was wrong with us.

Now we realize that the rhythm of our childhood years is the basic pattern of our entire life. The ups and downs of stable times, followed by fluid transitions, shape the contours of our adult lives.

In the past this normal feature of adult life was heavily camouflaged by the entrenched stability of the family, work institutions, churches, communities and the world itself. Although the social fabric around us is still fairly stable and moderately predictable, it is also looser, more fluid, and less able to assure us of lasting stability than it was not so very long ago. With every part of society shifting in constant change, there is little to buffer, hide or absorb the natural cycle of our lives. To sustain your life, you need to be able to live creatively with stable and unstable times. The key is in knowing that both will happen for you many times in the adult journey and understanding how to cooperate with the change process itself.

> *I have recently and reluctantly come to the conclusion that I am lost. Not just unsure that this is the right trail, but off any trail whatsoever. I find myself, figuratively, looking for footprints, broken twigs, any sign that someone has been over this ground ahead of me.*
>
> — Bill Bridges

Beginnings - Structures - Peaks

Committed
Outer Work
Achieving

Disoriented
Inner Work
Revitalizing

Endings - Transitions - Valleys

Understanding Life Chapters and Transitions

We are all the time putting our lives together and taking them apart – weaving and unraveling. When we are primarily weaving ourselves together, we are in a chapter – a time of relative stability, predictability and engaging challenge. When we are mainly unraveling or taking apart our story lines and our roles, we are in transition – a time of instability, shedding and entering the unknown.

Periods of stability and structure are the "chapters" of your life, times when – for the most part – life seems secure, purposeful, anchored, and goal-oriented. In a life chapter, the world seems mostly stable with plenty of opportunities to grow and live well. Our dominant behavior pattern is optimistic, engaged, and full of energy. Change seems like a controllable flow of resources and opportunities for fulfilling life's purpose. Performing in certain roles and succeeding in a variety of goals is a way to serve our greater sense of purpose.

Life chapters are about accomplishing something important with your life – reaching a goal, inventing a business, starting a career, raising a family – weaving your life together in some purposeful way. Our chapters will vary in duration; some will be long and others just a few short years.

- This is your *outer journey* into the world around you, where you face external challenges, threats and opportunities.

> *If one's destiny is shaped from within, then one has become more of a creator, has gained freedom. Here one acts as subject, author, creator.*
>
> — Allen Wheelis

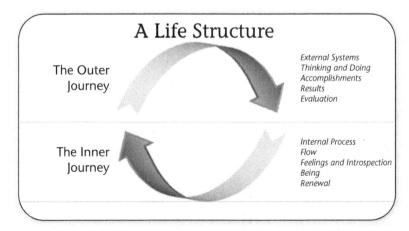

• These stable times provide you with *opportunities for continuous roles* (parent, leader, husband, volunteer within which you can live out a plan and produce results. You want to "do something" and arrive at success, recognition and happiness.

While life chapters are externalizations of the self – doings and happenings with explicit goals and objectives, *life transitions* are a pulling away from a chapter and a call to turn inward, to soul search, to unearth a new layer, to find a new sense of self. In this phase of life you engage in deconstructing an old self, shedding a 'skin of life', and in the midst of this you often experience the world as unreliable, chaotic, and punishing. You are likely to feel discouraged, have low energy, wonder *why me?*, and at least for a while feel pessimistic and confused about the future.

Human beings, by changing the inner attitudes of their minds, can change the outer aspects of their lives.

— William James

Sometimes you enter this territory intentionally, and many times you are caught off guard. When the events of life drop an abrupt change in your lap – a downsizing and loss of job, a financial blow, a divorce, or a major health challenge – you can easily loose your moorings and find yourself withdrawing from your usual, dependable coping mechanisms. A difficult shift may **draw you into a solitary space and time where you find yourself examining your whole life journey and asking the big questions – What now? With whom? Where? and more.**

In short, a life transition instinctively turns one inward and *demands* we disengage from much of life's "busyness"; our inner voices seem more reliable than outer signals. In this space we take apart the former chapter and our old ways of being; we evolve as a person, shedding one of life's veneers and eventually growing into a new layer of self, a new chapter, much like a butterfly when it cocoons. We call this *cocooning* because it is a time of rebirth filled with opportunities for transformation, amazing growth and renewal.

• This is the *inner journey* into your own identity, your being, longings, unlived dreams and core values.

• In a transition, you concentrate on developing a new layer of *your own inner self – the vital center of all renewal.* You awaken to new forces and callings within yourself.

*It is only when we
realize that life is
taking us nowhere
that it begins to
have meaning.*

— P.D. Ouspensky

• You discover new *possibilities for your life ahead.* This is a journey into your own capacity to redirect yourself – with new vision and courage – toward a future that will add meaning to your life. Transitions position you toward the future, with reduced attachment to the past. You are free to dream again, to take charge of your life, and to redefine the purpose of the next chapter of your life.

• Many transitions also provide you with social rites of passage, linking together the chapters of your life, so you can feel yourself "graduating" from one chapter of life into the next. These help you measure your lifelong journey.

To stay·renewed, we need to know how to manage both experiences: building successful external life chapters and discovering new internal resources through your transitions. Buddhist and Hindu cultures see life's polarities more clearly than we do in Western cultures. They see life as a cycle with up-time and down-time, neither of which is "better" than the other. Both experiences are natural, essential, and inevitable parts of the ever-renewing cycle of change. A snake can't grow a new skin on top of its old one, it has to shed the old one first and then begin anew. So it seems with us as well.

The Four Phases of Change
A Renewal Cycle

Map One

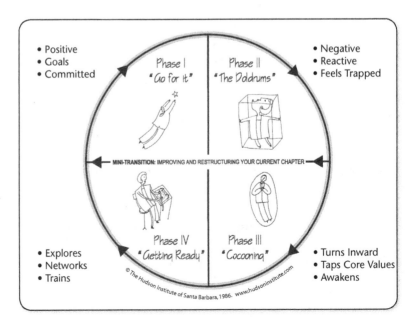

Our model views change and continuity as a ceaseless and sustained positive force in adult life. According to our model, adults today need to be thoroughly at ease managing both the chapters and transitions in life. We learn from all places in the change cycle, and the most basic lesson of our model is that there are no permanent arrival points, only a long and continuous journey as we navigate continuous change.

The human systems to which we belong (families, work organizations, communities and the larger world) also move through chapters and transitions. This enriches and complicates the picture further because we are not living on islands, but instead our individual experiences are embedded in all the important parts of our lives.

Change – rapid and constant, exhilarating and daunting – is the theme of our time. The metaphor of a wild rapids ride captures two qualities central to our mostly universal experience of this change phenomenon: a sense of chaotic power beyond our control coupled with a sense of energizing, thrilling possibilities. The rapids metaphor isn't merely external to us, it is internal as well. When we feel at home in the sea of change we are able to adapt to the flow – the intensity of the rapids, and we learn to navigate and anticipate the upcoming forks in the river.

Our journey through life can feel like a rapids ride, yet it flows in a cycle with recurring patterns of events and life tasks. The Cycle of Renewal moves from relatively stable periods – life chapters, to unstable periods – life transitions, and on to new life chapters. This Cycle, a continuous flow moving and changing throughout our lives, is shown in the diagram of Map1.

The Cycle of Renewal has four phases or time periods. Each phase has an organizing principle that defines it, along with tasks and activities to make it happen. Each phase proceeds in a clockwise direction, moving through the change process around the Cycle.

Our lives are a series of births and deaths: we die to one period and must be born to another. We die to childhood and are born to adolescence; to our high-school selves and (if we are fortunate) to our college selves; we die to our college selves and are born into the 'real' world; to our unmarried selves and into our married. To become a parent is birth to a new self for the mother and father as well as for the baby.

— Madeleine L'Engle

A Personal Journey

Barbara is an accomplished professional, a mother, wife, and advocate in her various communities. She has traveled the path of the Renewal Cycle a few times over the course of several decades and now, as she crosses into her sixties, she shares a story about her journey spanning her twenties into her later fifties weaving us through her many chapters and transitions, and offering us an up-close or an intimate glimpse into the four phases of the Cycle of Renewal.

I can still remember what I was wearing as I stood on the steps of New York's City Hall that classic November morning – a hot pink silk shantung jacket, an off-white slim skirt and matching blouse with a signature cameo, a perfect professional look for the perfect professional moment.

After almost a year of late nights, weekend-less weeks, and little more than cat-naps for the last 72 hours, I had done what promising junior associates do best: I had orchestrated a closing with military precision – signatures from the Mayor, the Governor, and the Secretary of the Treasury, and had carried briefcases for the best of them. Not only that, but I still looked pretty good and I felt terrific! The adrenaline was flowing. I was high, horribly so, on my own success.

The kid from Schenectady in me could hardly believe how perfect it felt standing on those steps, accepting accolades, and waiting for my black car to whisk me and my bags of perfect documents back to the office and then home for a long overdue weekend of "quality" time with my beautiful 2-year old. I was 28 with the world before me and, although I didn't know it at the time, I was "going for it"!

And then it happened.

One of the partners in my firm broke free from the informal celebration and pulled me aside. When I got back to the office, he asked, would I stop in to see his partner? He had a little something he needed help with. "A little something," what a transparent code! It meant I'd be in the office that weekend too.

There it was: my personal introduction to The Doldrums.

I was going someplace alright: I was going back to the office, still sleepless. My adrenaline was gone; fatigue was creeping through my arms and legs. My eyes were beginning to burn. I couldn't believe it. We couldn't even finish celebrating! What kind of a life had I gotten myself into?

I felt so trapped! From then on, the firm just wasn't the same. I tried to recapture the moment on the steps but I started to avoid, or at least dread, the most dramatic assignments. The city was still seductive. The black cars that too often picked me up in the suburbs before the early trains were running and brought me home after the last train at night still played their siren song. The dinners "on the client" in those chic haunts near the office were still so elegant. And, so, as much as I hurt inside, I stayed on, letting the voices in my head rule: "They can't make me quit!" And they couldn't! But neither could I.

I went on like that for almost two years, doing well professionally but dressing a little less well and denying, on the personal front, what I had so clearly discovered on that fine November morning.

One day a crack appeared in my wall of denial: A cold call from a headhunter. A brand name bank was starting to build an in-house legal department. It was a great chance to get in on the ground floor and my daughter was about to start school. I knew I would never see her if I kept working the way I had in those years. But, even then, I can't say I jumped at the opportunity. Instead, I simply forced myself to accept.

The change was dramatic and joyless! My dreams of partnership were over. My buddies were gone, still working too hard to even get together. If you wanted to see them, you had to be part of their game and, suddenly, I was not.

Instead, I was starting over, proving myself one more time. It was almost a year before I began to feel a platform beneath my feet again and see a future open up. I had no idea what I was doing taking all those long walks by the water, listening to jazz, and gardening. If you had told me I was cocooning, I would have been utterly mystified. But that's what I was doing, by the book, until the lightness gradually came back into my life!

I spent almost 23 years with that firm. Sometimes it filled me with energy and sometimes the roses were hard to smell. But gradually I learned to make little changes that made a difference. Mini-transitions in the flesh! I took on new clients with new personalities and new issues whenever the opportunity arose, and changed locations (downtown, uptown, downtown, and back again).

Each small turn of the dial kept things fresh for me. I'd start to sink into that "stuck" place and an opportunity would present itself. New clients, new work, new bosses, a new office, new people reporting to me, a new commute, a better coffee shop (one that served a fancy Belgian Chocolate with each fresh cup!) Each time, it was just enough change to reenergize me.

And then the inevitable happened. Just when I had my dream job and my dream client, my firm was merging and my job was to be moved half a continent away. I had more than my share of merger experience but this time was different. I was being torn in two. Part of me, the competitive and curious me, desperately wanted to make the move and stay in the game. Part of me knew that the time had come to begin to enjoy the dream retirement future my husband was already creating on our boat. And so, I took the leap.

Talk about change! One day, I was the general counsel to a major business with staff all across the country; the next I was aboard the boat as a staff of one: cooking, navigating, learning new knots, and taking my turn at the wheel. My well known mixed emotions were in high gear as I vacillated between wondering why I had waited all those years to do what was now consuming me and asking myself what on earth I had just done by abandoning my career!

And so, the cocooning commenced once more – this time in a gentler way, with the white noise of the engines to hypnotize, the sea grasses to soothe, and the weather to dictate the rhythm of the days. I had put away my watch and declined to make plans. I studied for the Coast Guard Captain's test. I got my coaching certification. I played with pastels. We cruised up and down the East Coast and I cooked with great abandon – whole flounder Savannah style cooked in a lock on the way through the Dismal Swamp canal. I couldn't make the stuff up. We drove cross country on a whim and saw the desert in bloom. Whenever I could, I babysat for my grandsons without worrying about work.

I was doing something completely new for me: unconsciously leaving space for things to happen. And happen they did!

Old friends started to call and ask for help thinking about what they should be doing in the wake of our company's most recent merger, and when they called forth the coach in me, it felt right. Another asked me to come and give a speech about my experiences as the only woman in the room for so many years. I had never been a speaker. I never enjoyed it in the least, but this time I was talking from the heart and sharing my message. Again, it felt right. Finally, I had started to write about things that had been on my mind for a long time and, when I did, the hours passed like minutes. I was experimenting with life and, I now see, "Getting Ready!"

There it was: my next experiment: coach, speaker, and writer. Let the Cycle begin again! Go for it!

But that is not the magic or the miracle of it all. The magic, the miracle, is that now I have a heightened sense of the rhythm of my life and an openness to the opportunity that change presents and the lightness that can follow.

And so, Barbara's journey through a series of chapters and transitions breathes life into the four phases of the Cycle of Renewal. Let's take a closer look:

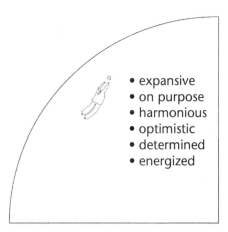

- expansive
- on purpose
- harmonious
- optimistic
- determined
- energized

PHASE ONE: "GO FOR IT" is the positive part of the life chapter where you seek to live your dream and – if all goes well – reach a sustainable plateau of success and well-being. Just like Barbara standing on the steps basking in her accomplishments in her first corporate leadership role, when you're in Phase 1, you feel expansive, on fire, passionate, on purpose and very much alive! You are mostly harmonious, optimistic and thoroughly determined. When you land upon the right dream, you feel electrified, energized and determined to make it happen. Your dream is your vision for how you really want to be at this time in your life, in this world – you are on course. If all goes well, your idealistic dreams lead to realistic planning and you launch your plan with action steps, timelines and endless revisions that keep you on course in Phase 1.

This is the phase that many love the most, and we often think it's supposed to last forever while just getting better and better – but just like the seasons, nothing lasts forever, and Phase 1 is no exception! Even when you are thoroughly committed to the course you've plotted, you are still likely to reach a plateau when much of your dream has been realized. The plateau is both a blessing and a curse. The blessing is the sweet success you've experienced in what is often a very long period of time. The curse is that even after tinkering and revising the dream, there comes a time when it just doesn't energize you anymore and you have to let go.

Barbara reached this crossroads when the dinners, the black cars and the promise of partner were not enough to keep her on track and aligned with her original plan. There's no way around it; sooner or later, even when you've succeeded at reaching your goals, you get flat and begin to feel a little bored with the whole picture that felt so 'spot on' just yesterday. Your energy wanes, you feel a little indifferent, and what was once 'the perfect dream' becomes something like an albatross hanging on your neck, and getting heavier and heavier.

At this point in the journey most of us experience two opposing sensations simultaneously: we feel an urge to let go and move on to a new challenge, and we believe we deserve to remain on this plateau for as long as possible, reaping the rewards of our hard work and finding small ways to improve it and make it last just a little longer.

There are important strategies that allow us to maximize our dream in this 'Go For It' phase, to extend our stay as long as we can; at the top of the list is the ability to create a work-life balance routine. There is plenty of evidence that we do our best in our most important roles in life when we are able to care for ourselves, managing our energy and finding a balance between work and leisure. A 'one string guitar' has only one tune to play and when the tune gets old, there is nothing else to rely on to refresh the 'concert'. The analogy is obvious – if you are invested in only one role in life, you limit the options and miss out on a whole lot of life!

Our greatest glory is not in never falling, but in rising every time we fall.

— Confucius

So eventually, the challenges wane, the routines become all too familiar, the small adjustments just don't work anymore and you begin to feel imprisoned by the very scenario you thought would lead to your eternal fulfillment. You are in "The Doldrums".

- out of sync
- trapped
- helpless
- sad
- defeated
- resistant

PHASE 2: "THE DOLDRUMS" is a down time, a protracted sense of decline, when you're not happy with your life chapter, but you don't think you can do much about it. It is not merely that you feel stuck or out of energy. The chapter of life you are in – with all its players and circumstances – seems stuck as well. When you're in Phase 2, the dream fades, your life routines become all too familiar, and there is growing dissonance between you and the other people in your chapter. You feel like you are in a predicament from which you can't extricate yourself, as if you were wounded, helpless, and without adequate resources to see ahead. Barbara found herself at this place when she started to consider jumping off the partnership track in her law firm. She didn't want it anymore; yet she couldn't stand the thought of letting go of the hard work, the dream, and all the trappings.

So as it goes in The Doldrums, Barbara's life chapter became heavy and out of sync. Her motivation decreased, her negativism

*To everything
there is a season...
a time to build,
a time to break
down, a time to
dance, a time to
mourn. A time to
cast away stones,
a time to gather
stones together.*

— Peter Seeger

likely increased, and she felt trapped in the very settings and activities that in the past fulfilled her. This is precisely the experience of all of us when we arrive in the Doldrums! We resist change because we don't know what to do to make things better, but in fact we are defensive and prickly much of the time. Unfortunately, we adults tend to remain in this phase longer than is often useful because we feel immobilized and at times victimized by forces beyond ourselves. We seem to naturally resist endings, tightening the grip on what we've known even when it hasn't served us particularly well. It's as though we would rather improve a broken chapter than enter into a period filled with unknowns. But often life isn't in our complete control and the unfamiliar comes knocking on our door, catching us off guard and unhinging us from important parts of our past.

Mighty life changes, planned or seemingly foisted upon us, inevitably stir within us the deep mystery of loss and grief. We've all experienced this at least once or twice along life's path – a parent dies, a long-term marriage comes to an end, a life-long professional identity is retired, the last child leaves home, a significant personal illness arrives as an unexpected visitor, or, like Barbara when the merger was announced – a long-term career took an unexpected turn. So for Barbara or any of us faced with one of these mighty life changes, our world is turned upside down overnight with little preparation and all of a sudden we are faced with a quick decisions to make 'on the fly' and plenty of unknowns!

While it is most common to feel stuck or trapped at times like this, you actually have only a couple of good choices: improve the script (if possible) and renew your current chapter of life, or end this chapter and begin a transition toward a very new chapter. Sometimes the choices are crystal clear – there's simply 'no going back', and many other times there are real options for making small adjustments that make a big difference. Whenever you are mired in The Doldrums, stay proactive and choose one of these paths before you find comfort in your discomfort and prolong the story.

One of the most important strategies for managing your stay in The Doldrums is NOTICING – noticing you are in The Doldrums, paying attention to how long you've been in this phase, focusing on any patterns relative to your visits to the Doldrums. You can't move on if you don't notice where you are! Some approaches to help you identify where you are in the Cycle: seek feedback from friends and colleagues who are willing to be frank with you; engage in some daily journaling and notice any patterns and common themes; chart the ups and downs of the past two or three years and develop a visual picture of your journey, pinpointing the patterns.

Life shrinks or expands in proportion to one's courage.

— Anais Nin

Mini-Transition

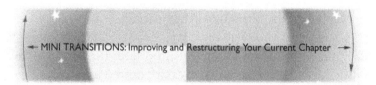

MINI TRANSITIONS: Improving and Restructuring Your Current Chapter

Most times what is called for in life are small changes, crafting new ways of staying closer to what matters most to you, getting back on track with a revised plan for the foreseeable future. It might be a new job, a new position in the old company, a visit to a marriage counselor, a change in location, carving out time for a lost pasttime, a new plan for time off and life balance routines – we call this a Mini-Transition, your short-cut across the Renewal Cycle and back to 'Go For It'. Ninety percent of the time, when you exhaust feeling sorry for yourself in the doldrums of a life chapter, you will try to fix the chapter. You do something you believe will correct the problems and get yourself back on course again. You strive to improve the chapter you are in.

Barbara's story includes several trips through 'The Doldrums' with a series of shortcuts back to 'Go For It' via the Mini-Transition route – she infused new energy and passion into her work by finding new clients, getting a new office location, adjusting her position inside the firm to take on new challenges, shifting her commute habits, and more. Each time these adjustments were just enough to allow for a longer stay in the current chapter.

A mini-transition is a small move; you've invested a lot of energy and money in creating and sustaining this chapter of your life - why not put some extra effort into making it last a little longer? In effect, you conduct a personal strategic plan, sorting out the assets from the liabilities. You keep the main themes, roles and characters of your chapter, but you make some significant changes as well.

A Mini-Transition is a time of strategic planning, renewing the current chapter of your life with new strategies to improve what's working and change what's not, introducing new options, and getting launched again. Mini-Transitions are a restructuring of what already exists in the service of improving it, and therefore are as essential as dramatic life transitions.

In short, if the Mini-Transition renews your chapter with resilience, hope, and challenge, you may stay in this chapter for a long time. But if the Mini-Transition does not produce these qualities and instead leaves you disappointed and discouraged, you have little choice but to move on to Cocooning.

I simply believe that some part of the human self or soul is not subject to the laws of time and space.

— Carl Jung

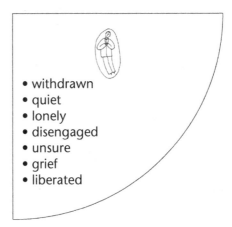

• withdrawn
• quiet
• lonely
• disengaged
• unsure
• grief
• liberated

PHASE THREE: "COCOONING". Sooner or later, every life chapter fades and becomes unworkable. Just like Barbara, you make as many small adjustments (Mini-Transitions) that work for as long as possible until the alterations simply don't do the trick anymore. You've extracted all that's joyful and meaningful out of the current chapter – it might be a career that no longer fits you, a role as mother that is mostly completed in the full-time fashion, a business you are ready to sell, a marriage that no longer works – while particulars vary, the reality is the same. Remember that for any of us, there are only a handful of times in our adult lives when we are compelled to make radical changes that move us into the lower half of the Cycle of Renewal and into transformative *life transition* territory. We venture into this territory of the Cycle when we take a courageous leap of faith or some external crisis pushes us to the precipice and we slowly begin a walk down a new road in our adult journey.

Cocooning is a detachment from the chapter that no longer works or was fully used up. Cocooning is taking an emotional "time out" to heal, reflect, and discover new directions for your life, eventually leading you toward renewal and revitalization. Cocooning begins in the pain of The Doldrums, but becomes a full-time preoccupation when you say goodbye to your old life. It takes an ending to find a new beginning. Within the "goodbye" is liberation from the roles and preoccupations that occupied you for such a long time.

Before you tell your life what you intend to do with it, listen for what it intends to do with you.

— Parker Palmer

You grieve the loss of the chapter, the roles, the whole structure of what you had, and you feel as though your whole life has ended. Even though this grieving began as you neared the end of your stay in The Doldrums, now you feel almost burdened with yourself as you fully enter the stage of Cocooning.

Barbara describes her dramatic shift as she writes: *"One day, I was the general counsel to a major business with staff all across the country; the next I was aboard the boat as a staff of one: cooking, navigating, learning new knots, and taking my turn at the wheel."*

Learning to tie knots was just the beginning of Barbara's Cocooning process. When you Cocoon, you take stock of your life, create an inner conversation with yourself, and tap into your core values and feelings. Just as a caterpillar cannot anticipate becoming a butterfly when it enters its cocoon, adults feel awkward and lost at the beginning of a major transition. You wander around for a time, looking in on your life without a clear sense of the new anchors and values you want to hold closest to you now. You lose control over much of your life when you enter the lower half of the Cycle and make a big life transition, and then slowly, over time, you gain inner trust and a new thirst to grow.

People in Cocooning are quiet at times, withdrawn, often emotional, and generally unsure. You don't have to stop living or working to cocoon, although the less energy you invest in your various roles, the sooner you are likely to be fed and replenished by your real self. Just as pruning a rose bush leads to a more robust plant, so cocooning enables people to discover new part of themselves.

Disengagement is a time for *being*, not *doing*. In time, people who are devoted to working through loss find amazing inner resources they didn't realize they had. With healing and renewal, reintegration with the external world begins again.

To Cocoon is to be gifted with new strength and a challenging engaging script from the inside-out. Cocooning has more to do with the regeneration of positive feelings of self-regard and spiritual trust beyond yourself than with "doing" anything. There is no shortcut on this path. Cocooning usually takes many months, and in the end, it leads to a profound inner renewal of energy, purpose and hope. The result of a stay in Cocooning is a new script – the beginning of a new "story" for your next chapter of life and this time. New dimensions and layers of the self will be chosen, like the skin of a new snake, to fit current dreams and values and to accommodate current social conditions and opportunities. The dark night of the soul fades into morning's sunrise, and the cocoon breaks apart paving the way for the journey ahead.

At no time do we need strategies more than when we are in this Cocooning phase. It's so thoroughly counter-intuitive to take time out in order to move into something new and vital, that it's an unnatural state of being for us. The very concept of reflection is largely foreign in today's fast paced world. Cocooning requires reflection; it takes time, and it requires we suspend our drive toward actions and planning, and demands we create some structures that allow us to do this important work. The picture of sitting at a sidewalk café in a walled city somewhere in Tuscany comes to mind as the perfect setting for this work, but let's face it, few of us have that opportunity! We need to keep paying the bills and attending to our responsibilities in life while we make space to Cocoon.

How do we create ways to Cocoon? Develop a daily practice – maybe it's an hour long walk at the beginning or end of each day – something that you engage in day in and day out while you are in this phase. Write, journal, and doodle – take 15 minutes a day to jot down all of your thoughts or build mind maps that help you walk through the maze of your current situation. Go on a retreat – a weekend, a week, a month, find a simple retreat setting where you can be alone for long periods of time, or just

I don't know what your destiny will be, but one thing I know: the only ones among you who will be really happy are those who have sought and found how to serve.

— Albert Schweitzer

a simple vacation without scheduled events to experiment and let your inner interests surface, or treating Sunday as "the day of abject indolence."

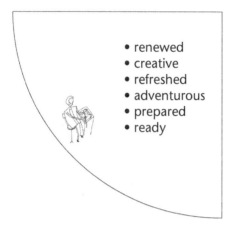

- renewed
- creative
- refreshed
- adventurous
- prepared
- ready

Creativity is the process of bringing something new into being.

— Mary Rollé

"Many – far too many – aspects of life which should also have been experienced lie in the lumber room among dusty memories. Sometimes, even, they are glowing coals under grey ashes." – C. Jung

PHASE FOUR: "GETTING READY" is a time of rebirth, play and experimentation. It is a time for new learning, new relationships, networking, and testing new ways of being – all leading to a launching of your next chapter. This is a bit like being in school again, preparing for the rest of your life. In this phase you are mostly optimistic, dreamy, creative and confident. You experiment, network and invest in learning, and you are very eager to explore new skill sets and ways of thinking. It's at this stage in the Cycle that you slowly begin to link your renewed self with the possible scenarios for your life in the world that surrounds you.

Barbara leaves us in the middle of this phase when she tells us she's experimenting again and looking ahead to life beyond the law firms and corporate offices; and she gives us a peek into her experiments – writing, speaking, coaching. This is the work of this phase – experimenting without agenda, without judgment, with a final outcome in place!

Just like Barbara, it is here you are trying on new roles as possibilities without moving to any long-term decisions. This is as it should be – we have few times in our adult journey to experiment again, try on new possibilities for the next long chapter ahead; don't rush this process, allow it to unfold over a few months.

Sooner or later, you discover some path that feels right for a new life chapter, and the Cycle begins again. You become heady, optimistic, refreshed, ready, and prepared. And, you also have a touch of sadness because you are leaving the freedom of this phase of 'Getting Ready' and moving into the responsibilities that come with the beginning of the Cycle anew.

When you find yourself in this phase there are some useful strategies and tips to keep in mind. First, according to Webster, the definition of 'experiment' is *trying out new ways of doing things*. This is important to remember – trying out – and taking your time as you try out new possibilities. We tend to rush ourselves when we get to this place in the Cycle, and we often hear a voice on our shoulder whispering *'OK, now it's time to get this right, to get on with things, hurry up, don't waste time, what will others think."*

Give yourself a timeframe and commit to experimenting within that timeframe, don't jump on the first thing you try, allow yourself the luxury of discovering, evaluating, and slowly landing on what seems just right. Barbara may never become a sailing expert or go on the speaking circuit, but for now, she's giving herself permission to try it out!

The continuous flow of the four phases is how we grow and develop through our adult years. That's what makes it the Cycle of Renewal. It's something like a river moving along through all kinds of weather, through all the seasons, through all kinds of terrain and environments. Each cycle has two parts: the stable life chapter being the themes and activities you knit together as a chapter of your life, and the transition being an unraveling – a letting go followed by the discovery of new themes and a new layer of you that you want for the next chapter of your life. And on and on it goes throughout our years. The story of Stephen and Susan sheds a little light on some of this journey from the perspective of a couple:

It is only by living completely in this world that one learns to have faith.

— Dietrich Bonhoeffer

A Story of Stephen and Susan
From Doldrums to Cocooning as a Couple

The lives of Stephen and Susan reveal the dynamics of both parts of the Renewal Cycle of Change. They have been married for nineteen years. With three children, they have lived in four different locations across the U.S. as Stephen climbed the ladder of his career. Although each move felt like a tidal wave to Susan, who hated to leave friends and school systems, Stephen strongly felt that the number one priority was reaching his peak so the family could benefit from financial security and stability. That's not the way it worked out.

Before Stephen was six months into his fourth management job, in Chicago, he was summarily fired. His superiors accused him of being autocratic, ego driven, lacking in empathy and listening skills, and fundamentally unable to collaborate with his workforce. Stephen was suddenly unemployed – he was crushed on the inside and enraged. Although he immediately tried to locate new management positions, no one seemed interested in him. His seething temperament and overeager style got him nowhere in the job interviews he landed.

That was only the beginning of the bottom falling out of his life. Now that Stephen's career was derailed, Susan insisted on evaluating their marriage and family life. "I can't take it any more," she said. "We haven't seen much of you, Stephen, for a decade. You just work, work, work. And then we move so you can work some more. I know we need money, but I won't live this way any more. Jill is sixteen, and she's been off track for more than a year now – seriously. She barely knows who you are. Johnny is thirteen and so much wants to be close to you, but you're never here – and when you are, we all know you're just getting rested so you can get back to work. I've got a part-time job, but I also manage the home and the family, and I just won't do it alone any more."

Stephen was at the end of a chapter of his life. When he was younger, he had designed his work roles and career path to fit his life as a twenty-year-old. He defined his life through his work as his father had done. But now the messages from his employer, wife and teenage children, along with his inner anger and outmoded management style add up to time for a life transition.

He took time off to reevaluate things, and in the process he learned a lot about himself and his preferred life direction. He went on some long trips with his teenagers, and got closer to their concerns and hurts. He and Susan joined a couple's group to look at ways to grow their marriage. He even came to wonder why he had spent so many years trying to be someone he never really was. At home, he and his son Johnny built a new addition onto the house.

Stephen developed daily rituals – going on walks, meeting friends, cooking meals, and planning weekend getaways. He also became involved at his church with the family camping programs. Meanwhile, Susan invested more time in her work, both to develop her career further and to provide necessary funding for the transition.

Little by little, Stephen caught up with his own depth and breadth. He found a job near his home that paid fairly well, although not nearly as much as the career track he had been on. But his new work engaged him in teamwork, with ongoing training and balanced well with his new roles in the family. When his transition ended, Stephen had a new script, a new story, and a life plan that deepened his journey as a human being by reevaluating his priorities, time commitments, values and roles. He and his family were on their way again.

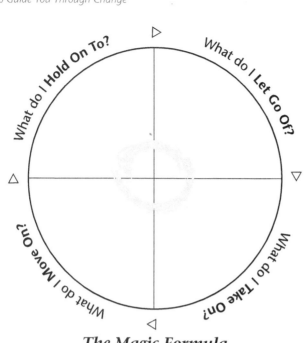

The Magic Formula

Knowing how to move yourself around the Renewal Cycle of Change is like staying in shape; it empowers you to be at your best at all times, whether you are assuming leadership roles while structuring, or shedding those roles because they have become stale habits, or unavailable, in a transition.

There is a magic formula of eight words that will keep this Map close to you: **Hold On, Let Go, Take On, Move On.** As you consider your best choices for composing your life, sort out each option into one of these categories:

Hold on to what is valuable to you and important in the interconnectedness of your life. Hold on to what is working in your life. Never trash everything. There is always something precious and gem-like to take with you and to build upon in the journey ahead. The older you are, the greater your reservoir of experience for finding diamonds and rubies. Always hold on to what you value in yourself and your relationships before you do anything else.

Let go of what's not working, of what is worn out, of what doesn't belong to your future. In our society it is practically un-American to let go of anything you accumulate, from things to habits; but letting go of what is dysfunctional in you and your human settings is a prerequisite to taking on healthy options for the future. You can't

I have no way of knowing what results my actions will have.... My only sure reward is in the depth of my response.

— Hugh Prather

truly take on new directions until you let go of the excess baggage in your life. Just as pruning old branches encourages vibrant new growth, you have to risk letting go to gain freedom for moving on into new possibilities.

Take on new skills, attitudes, and resources for creating the next chapter of your life. Taking on involves learning, training, growing, and becoming. It is an invitation to awaken to more of yourself and to take advantage of the world as a veritable campus awaiting your self-directed study program. Learn to evolve!

Move on is what happens when you hold on, let go, and take on. New paths appear. Your sail feels the wind as your rudder guides you to new destinations. You feel yourself on a new pilgrimage you believe in. You find yourself at a new beginning – fresh, ready, and eager. You are on your way.

And this too will end, as the Renewal Cycle of Change goes on and on.

Your Turn!

1. Are you at several places on the Renewal Cycle, with parts of you open to launching, while other parts are complaining? Your various roles will always be spread around the Cycle, but you, yourself, the conscious center of the person that is living your life, are at predominantly one place in the Cycle. Write down in your notebook where you think you are in your various roles, such as spouse, worker, parent, friend and community leader, etc. Then indicate the approximate place you are as a whole person or self, at this time in your life. You can find your central place in the Renewal Cycle by your feelings and the life tasks that engage you.

2. Which of the four phases of the Renewal Cycle are you most familiar and comfortable with? (Go for It, The Doldrums, Cocooning, or Getting Ready for the Next Chapter) Least familiar with? What you would like that you don't now know?

3. Leaving home in your late teens or twenties to begin the adult years is your first adult transition. Describe your experience below:

– What was your cocooning experience like when you left home? Were you escaping or seeking?

– When you began to explore possibilities for launching the first chapter of your adult life, what were your options and considerations, and how did you get ready for making it successful?

– Who were the primary characters in the first chapter of your adult life?

– What was your vision or dream for that first chapter of your adult life, and what action plans did you follow to live your dream?

– What did you learn from leaving home – your first adult transition?

4. Some people have trouble seeing a transition as a positive force in their life. What words do you associate with a "transition"? What *positive developments* might accompany disruptive events like the following?

– A friend finds herself jobless after fifteen years in a corporate setting.

– A colleague decides to leave the rat race to live on less.

– A close friend leaves his or her marriage.

– Your mother suffers a stroke.

– You give birth to your first child and all of your old notions about work and goals seem irrelevant.

5. What is a *successful* transition, for you? Have you ever had one? If so, what characteristics in your experience made it successful?

6. Describe the finest chapter in your life thus far. What makes it "the finest"? How can you have these qualities in your next chapter?

Chapter Five

Map 2

A Deliberate Life

If you were alone in the universe with no one to talk to, no one which to share the beauty of the stars, to laugh with, to touch, what would be your purpose in life? It is other life, it is love, which gives your life meaning. This is harmony. We must discover the joy of each other, the joy of challenge, the joy of growth. — Mitsugi Saotome

The Whole Person

We have now walked through the each phase in the Cycle of Renewal. We may have long and satisfying chapters interspersed with a few major transitions over the course of our lives or we may experience many, many changes, surprises and crisis that require a walk around the cycle on several occasions. Whatever our individual circumstance, there is a predictable flow in the change process, a cycle we can dependably return to as a compass when life feels 'out of control' or particularly perplexing – a continual process of knitting together or unraveling, and then beginning again. **If you know where you are, at any time, in your heart of hearts, you will know how to proceed, what to look forward to, and what capabilities and skills to call on and build for the new journey.**

It's not enough to be busy. So are the ants. The question is: what are you busy about?

— Henry David Thoreau

Here's a graphic depiction of these elements of the Whole Person:

© The Hudson Institute of Santa Barbara, 1986.

At the center of the continually-evolving journey is the ongoing Cycle of Renewal.

The second ring contains the Passion and Values that ground us on our journey. The third ring includes the ever-changing Roles and Systems we engage in throughout life. The fourth ring symbolizes the broader life journey spanning from our earliest adult years through our elder chapters. The outer circle is the ongoing learning and unlearning required to navigate life's choices and changes.

The whole person includes our sense of purpose and passion, the priorities of the many roles and systems in our lives, our place in the cycle of life and the developmental journey, the learning agenda we are engaged in and, of course, our location on the Renewal Cycle of Change.

A Deliberate Life:
Living With Passion And Purpose

The purpose lens (the darkened ring in the illustration) helps you locate your deep energy and passion for the destinations you want to pursue. Yesterday's passions seldom serve tomorrow's goals, so you ask yourself "what motivates me the most at this

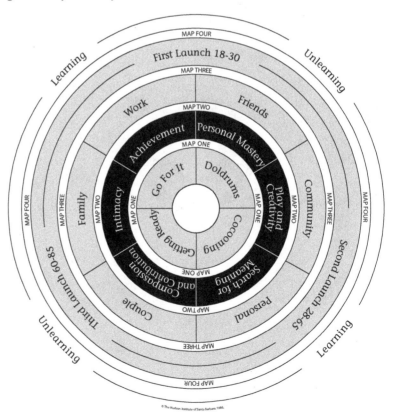

© The Hudson Institute of Santa Barbara, 1998.

time in my life to be the best I can be?" "What's most important to me at this time in the journey?" That's the fuel for your life and for the chapter ahead.

We all know people living in the past, such as the physician who retires and then returns to sit in the office each day because that's all he knows; the mother who never stops parenting. Living backward instead of leaning into the future means clinging to old passions without a sense of new possibilities. There is no need to lose our passion and sense of purpose half way through the adult journey, but often this happens because we are living out of yesterday's plans. As we move through life's journey we shift our priorities, our sense of purpose, our script for living, and if we are consciously engaged in this process we are also shifting our deepest sense of purpose – our fire for tomorrow.

Some life crises and a handful of predictable, yet breathtaking life events seem to naturally lead us to the doorway of purpose – the deeper questions of *"Why am I on this earth? What matters most to me at this time in my life? What's it all about?"* We've all encountered these turning points and passages. My first was in my early twenties when my closest childhood friend died in a car accident and all of a sudden, life's assumptions went out the window as I struggled to make sense out of existence just as I was entering the adult terrain. Her death brought me face-to-face with all of the questions about life – what am I here to do and be, what's important to me now, who and what matters most to me, and more. Many years later my passage into parenthood tapped another layer of purpose making – overnight, with the birth of my first child, the world was viscerally more alive, vastly more complex and blissfully purposeful.

And yet another turning point as I left my thirties decade – my father died, and this event more than any I'd encountered in my adult journey turned me inward on a long quest to come to terms with what was most purposeful in my life.

For all of us, our uniquely personal set of life events and predictable passages offer the invitation to ask bigger and deeper questions in order to sustain ourselves through major shifts and changes and sudden unexpected circumstances. Slowly,

---

Passion is a state of love and hunger.

— Gregg Levoy

with each successive change, we deepen the conversation with ourselves and cultivate our evolving sense of purpose.

Getting in Touch with Your Current Passions and Values

What you want for your life at thirty-five is seldom what you wanted at twenty, and won't likely be what you have in mind at fifty-five. Passions and priorities change as life evolves.

When we began studying how lives evolve in the adult years, we examined hundreds of biographies of twentieth century successful adults. We found that many measured their lives with six different basic values or passions – often in combination with one another. These six core values compete for our loyalty and passionate commitment throughout the life course, and we often shift gears through the adult years from familiar, accomplished passion areas to less familiar, attractive, and energized values:

> **Personal Mastering** – Know Thyself
> **Achievement** – Reach Your Goals
> **Intimacy** – Love and Be Loved
> **Play and Creativity** – Follow Your Intuition
> **Search for Meaning** – Spiritual Integrity
> **Compassion and Contribution** – Leave a Legacy

Each of these passions and values draws upon a different source of our human energy, and we have the capacity to tap all six passions, in various combinations, throughout the lifecycle, to sustain vitality and purpose. Too often we lock ourselves into the passions and values of our young adult years, and burn out during midlife, losing our zest for life. A better approach is to keep evaluating your priorities and preferences, to be sure that you are marching to your own drumbeats, empowered by the values you most honor at that time in your life.

Your passions are your internal energy source, the fire or determination you have for reaching some destination up ahead. They tell you why you are on this journey and what you want from life. They are your push and your pull. Find your passion for living this chapter of you life – and it will begin to unfold.

Our Six Adult Passions

Each chapter during your adult years has a different value base from previous ones. Your priorities change. Your expectations shift, particularly during life transitions. You create new preferences and ways to spend your time.

Core Values
Map Two

When everyone around you says you can't. When everything you know says you can't. Dig deeper within yourself and you find that you can.

— Mark Elliot Sacks

Map Two

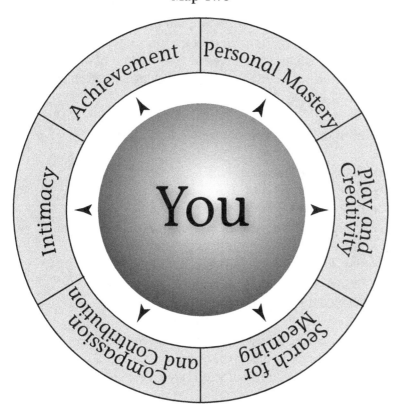

Most life chapters are built upon three or four of these passions. How would you sort out and prioritize these six in relationship at this time in your life? Browse through this section to gain a sense of all six passions and how they function. Pull out your journal or notebook and experiment with rank ordering (1-6)

the passions today or for the next chapter of your life. Or, write notes in a format that works for you. Concentrate on how you would engage today or in your next chapter with your top three or four passions.

Core Value One: Personal Mastery: *Claiming Yourself*

Identity, confidence, self-reliance, self-esteem, positive sense of self, personal boundaries, compassion for self, courage.

The Question: *Who am I at this time in my life?*

The Quest: Developing our sense of self is a lifelong endeavor at best, but there are times in the adult journey when this becomes a passion for us. Our earliest passage into adulthood naturally invites this quest as we seek to distill our identity separate from parents, family and old social structures. It seems to naturally emerge as a quest again somewhere midway along the journey when we've invested heavily in a handful of roles that have begun to lose their luster and it's time to shape a new identity.

Ways to increase personal power and mastery:

- Be assertive and clear
- Try out new ways of being
- Take good care of yourself
- Spend time with healthy people who sustain resilience
- Test your leadership abilities in new domains
- Stay committed to your personal goals
- Follow through on your commitments to self
- Balance the important parts of your life
- Engage in self reflective activities
- Hire a coach, spend some time in therapy
- Join an interest group that supports your goals
- Read works by Anthony Storr, Parker Palmer, John Schuster, Richard Leider, Pema Chodron, Thomas Moore

Core Value Two: Achievement: *Proving Yourself*

Reaching goals, working, winning, having ambition, doing, seeking recognition, conducting, organizing, leading, acquiring, becoming, getting results.

> *Never doubt that a small group of thoughtful committed citizens can change the world. Indeed, it is the only thing that ever has.*
>
> — Margaret Mead

The Question: *How far can I go, how much can I achieve on this path?*

The Quest: Successful achievement is most often measured and manifested in our work roles and all that comes with our work, although it can also manifest in our volunteer roles, our family roles, and even our creative ventures. This core value is a driving force in the first half of our adult journey and it's closely linked to the value of personal mastery. It's what we are up to when we land on a career area that fits our being, that brings us joy – and then the climb begins, to achieve, live into the work, take it to new levels and enjoy the fruits of our labor. This is most often the work of our early years. This same value seems to re-emerge in our later years again when we are ready to try something new, when we've shed some of the old demands and roles of the past and we are interested in climbing a new mountain (and not necessarily by taking the shortest path straight up, either!). There is a growing body of literature suggesting the women are particularly drawn to a new adventure later in life, and this draws us toward achievement.

> *Without love the acquisition of knowledge only increases confusion and leads to self-destruction.*
>
> — Krishnamurti

Ways to pursue Achievement:

- Set and maintain clear goals
- Have a plan to support the goals
- Have ways to measure your successes
- Join networks in your goal areas
- Stay in 'learning mode'
- Evaluate frequently
- Seek feedback
- Stay organized
- Develop self-reflective practices
- Find support in like-minded achievers
- Ready writings of Warren Bennis, Rosabeth Moss Kanter, Margaret Wheatley, Buckingham, and more

Core Value Three: Intimacy: *Sharing Yourself*

Loving, being intimate, caring, making relationships work, touching, bonding, feeling close, nesting, coupling, partnering, parenting, being a friend.

The Question: *What are the relationships I value most in my life and how do I invest in seeking, enjoying and sustaining those relationships?*

The Quest: Freud reminded us that work and love are the two essential elements of our adult years, and since his writings we've learned how important intimate connections are to our well-being throughout the journey. We need four or five good friends whom we are invested in sustaining and relishing; we seem to flourish in intimate relationships with our spouse or life partner; we revel in our role as parents and enjoy the unfolding of the relationship over time; and we know that touching is simply basic to life itself. Our challenge is in sustaining these intimate bonds – it takes time, skill, commitment and practice, and there's little teaching that promotes our understanding of this terrain.

Ways to pursue intimacy:

- Be a good friend
- Speak from the heart
- Give without gain
- Learn by asking
- Face conflict and seek solutions
- Speak the truth
- Be reliable
- Ritualize important celebrations and events
- Offer intimacy and risk rejection
- Read writings of Harville Hendrix, Ruth Morehouse & David Schnarf, John Gottmen, Jennifer Louden

Core Value Four: Play and Creativity: *Expressing Yourself*

Being imaginative, intuitive, playful, spontaneous, original, expressive, humorous, artistic, celebrative, re-creative, curious and non-purposive.

The Question: *What might creativity unleash and reveal in me?*

The Quest: "Creativity and play are an expression of spontaneity and joy, which are particularly plentiful in the last half of a transition. Creativity and play are sources of positive energy, full of optimism and promise. They tap a powerful life force that seeks new forms of human expression. Spontaneous play and creativity

> *Our main motivation for living is our will to find meaning in life.*
>
> — Viktor Frankl

are regenerative forces in our bodies and lives and important to our ongoing resilience and vitality. Few adults have enough play in their lives." Frederic M. Hudson, *The Adult Years*

Ways to pursue play and creativity:

- Take a class (dance, improvisation, art, singing, acting) that is all new material for you
- Practice small acts of creativity at home (make your own flower arrangements, cook from a new menu, set the table in a new way, paint a room a bold color)
- Play with clay, it does wonders for the soul
- Take walks regularly
- Spend time with fun friends
- Laugh
- Read the writings on creativity by Gene Cohen, Julia Cameron, Mihaly Csikszentmihalyi, Edward de Bono, Roger von Oech

Core Value Five: Search for Meaning: *Integrating Yourself*

Finding wholeness, unity, integrity, peace, an inner connection to all things, spirituality, trust in the flow of life, inner wisdom, a sense of transcendence, bliss.

The Question: *What do I feel?*

The Quest: This value naturally surfaces at every turning point in our lives. It is in letting go and saying goodbye, in the grieving and mourning, that we face the big questions of meaning. As Victor Frankl wrote, "Each man is questioned by life, and he can only answer to life by answering for his own life."

Ways to pursue Search for Meaning:

- Take long walks in contemplative places
- Seek out sacred spaces
- Journal
- Go on a retreat to a new place, all alone
- Create a regular meditation practice
- Read the works of Victor Frankl, Parker Palmer, Pema Chodron, James Hollis, Angeles Arrien, Richard Leider

If you want to lift yourself up, Lift up someone else.

— Booker T. Washington

Core Value Six: Compassion & Contribution: *Giving of Yourself*

Helping, feeding, reforming, leaving the world a better place, bequeathing, being generative, serving, volunteering, social and environmental caring, improving the world.

The Question: *What is my legacy? What will live on well after my death?*

The Quest: To find meaningful ways to contribute to the larger world, to make a difference in ways that are aligned with your own values.

Ways to pursue Compassion & Contribution:

- Do a good deed, anonymously
- Confront dying (write a letter to self)
- Simplify, replacing acquisition with divestiture
- Support a cause, important to you
- Pursue peace at every level of your life
- Join a volunteer effort for a day (Habitat for Humanity, etc)
- Read the works of Sister Theresa, Albert Schwietzer, Eleanor D. Roosevelt, Martin Luther King, Jimmy Carter, Marian Wright Edelman, Margaret Sanger, Nelson Mandela, Marc Freeman

Passionate Destinations

Your values are your compass for guiding your journey into your next chapter. They will point you toward what matters most to you. What are some of the destinations you want from your passions at this time in your life? Have you carefully considered how you want your next chapter to evolve? Take the top three or four passions that you want to direct your next chapter of life and construct a script for it, keeping you at the growing and learning 'edge' of your development.

Here's how thirty-five year old Mary articulates her next chapter through the lens of the most important passions and values in her life:

At the top of my values list at this time in my life are Intimacy, Contribution and Compassion, and Achievement. I'm thirty-five, I've climbed some ladders and they haven't all been up against the wall I had in mind. I've learned plenty along the way and I'm clearer than ever that I want a new kind of career that gives me deeper satisfaction, I want to build a stronger community of friends and I'm ready to give back in some small, regular and meaningful ways in my community. I want to form three deep and long lasting friendships in the next two years with my "intimacy" focus; My dad recently died from cancer and it really got me asking some big questions and noticing how important it is to give back in life. I want to volunteer on a regular basis with my local Hospice organization in my "compassion and contribution" focus; and finally, the biggest step -- I am ready to complete my MBA with my "achievement" focus so I can move into a leadership role in the right kind of organization within the next five years.

> *The more faithfully you listen to the voice within you, the better you will hear what is sounding outside. Only he who listens can speak.*
>
> —Dag Hammarskjold

Your Turn
How do you Count What Counts?

What are your measuring sticks, your private ways of counting success through life: Money? Position? Acquisitions? Status? Power? Authority? Career Success? Titles? Ability to Help Others? Family? Successful Parenting? Strong Friendships? Sexual Prowess? Travel? Integrity? Caring Influence? Spirituality?

This is an important question to face into and answer for yourself. We are not always conscious of the measuring sticks we use and drawing these into your awareness may be enough to make you decide to take some new approaches in the chapter ahead!

Choose your top five approaches from the following list. What are your measuring sticks for the next chapter of your life, in the next few years?

- The accumulation of money and things
- The validation and respect of others for your accomplishments
- The love and intimacy that comes from sustaining strong relationships
- The success of parenting good, productive, value-based children

- The success and effectiveness of your work life
- The ability to have fun and invest in your pastimes, hobbies and sports
- The strength to follow your beliefs, your spiritual path
- The willingness to join causes you believe in, to make a lasting contribution
- Others:

What is Your Life Purpose, Today?

Whenever you consult life's compass within yourself, it points toward the current purpose of your life. Your values, deep energy, and passionate destinations are all wrapped up into a profound sense of purpose, pulling you ahead into more of yourself, through the chapters of your life. This sense of purpose is like a vibrant channel, an illuminated path, a personal calling.

Your emerging purpose is much more than a simple set of goals. It is your compelling reason for being alive. It is your raison d'être, your personal and social version of inalienable rights. It is a pursuit of excellence beyond your reach, a sense of manifest destiny, an unstoppable drive.

It measures an era of your life by defining your central themes, context, and basic beliefs. It is essential, if adults are to be alive in a world of flux and complexity, that they have within themselves a clear sense of purpose – to measure the flow of external change by the abiding values of internal meaning.

In your notebook, write out a statement of purpose for the next chapter of your life. Keep your statement simple, succinct, poetic, and empowering. It can connect your top three or four passions to destinations you want to travel toward in your next chapter.

Begin with this phrase: *"My purpose, for the next chapter of my life, is to…*

Chapter Six

Map 3

Life's Assignments

A human being is part of the whole, called by us 'Universe'; a part limited in time and space. He experiences himself, his thoughts, and feelings as something separated from the rest – a kind of optical delusion of his consciousness. This delusion is a kind of prison for us, restricting us to our personal desires and to affection for a few persons nearest to us. — Albert Einstein

---

Life's Assignments – Balancing the Roles & Systems in Your Life

As adults we need to feel effective within the systems we embody. Just as a fish cannot live without water to swim in, we cannot live without the systems we're in and the contexts they provide for us. Our lives are *embedded* in systems through the roles we play in them. Our spheres and systems shape the way we think and feel, provide us with arenas for our fulfillment, and program us with demands and expectations.

I remember when I was in the 'thick' of parenting and spending a lot of time in children-centered environments – soccer fields, basketball games, art classes, school outings and more. Adults would inevitably come up to me and say 'Oh, are you Charlie's mom?' And quickly our conversation would drift into talk of Charlie, his friends and my role as his mother! In my professional role when I was thoroughly immersed in my work as a psychologist, friends and acquaintances would often introduce me to others as 'Yes, she is a psychologist', and the conversation would invariably turn to something in the psychological realms. Today, as a leader of a learning organization and a partner of a beloved spouse with Alzheimer's, I find myself again being introduced with reference to my roles more than as simply Pam. This is the experience most of us have – our most dominant roles at any time along life's course can easily become who we are if we allow it to be so.

At The Hudson Institute we underline the essential nature and perspective of a whole person. As whole persons we transcend our many roles while remaining embedded in these identities as well. Our role investments change as we develop and move through life; the shifts are sometimes planned and other times thrust upon us like a bucket of freezing cold water. And those of us who've been surprised when hit with the chill and shock of the freezing water, learn the tough lesson that we often become too attached to our roles and lose the connection to our deeper self. The self transcends the roles, incorporates the roles, balances them, and offers us solace and perspective when we are hit with a splash of reality through a loss, downsizing, firing, empty nest, a leaving home, or end of a much loved role.

It's true that some roles are simply more powerful than

All the world's a stage, and all men and women merely players. They have their exits and entrances; and one man in his time plays many parts.

— William Shakespeare

What a strange machine man is! You fill him with bread, wine, fish and radishes, and out of him comes sighs, laughter and dreams.

— Nikos Kazantzakis

others. Some roles demand so much of our time and attention that we slowly lose sight of our core 'self' and begin to believe we are that role – a leader, a physician, an attorney, a professor, a mother, or a politician. We become lopsided and out of touch with other important dimensions of our whole being. The longer we remain heavily invested in this one role, the harder it is to construct or rebuild a sense of self that's greater than one's role.

So what's the alternative, the solution to this standard plight of adulthood – the lopsided life? Most importantly, it's about the power of purpose – developing a sense of your values and your beliefs. Our purpose will change over the decades, but a grounding in our sense of purpose at all points along the journey keeps us focused on self with a healthier perspective on the roles we choose to invest in along the journey.

How do we view our Roles?

First, notice where you spend your time and what gets most of your attention over the course of a day, a week, a month of your current life chapter. Then notice how you feel about the time you devote to this role – are you passionate, alive, and thoroughly invested in this role? Or, are you grumbling, resentful, feeling imprisoned by the requirements of the role that consumes a good deal of your waking hours?

Next, notice the roles you are drawn to, but just can't find the time (our default excuse) or energy to devote to them. Maybe you are a leader inside your division and this consumes most of your time; yet, as you look at the other roles in your life, you are drawn to the parenting role and your two young kids. But there's the harsh reality of time – there is not enough, and the leadership role simply demands the lion's share of your attention. So you rationalize, you make up some excuses you can live with: "I'm supporting the overall family mission", "This is a temporary dilemma that will sort out next year", "This is what my company demands of everyone and I can't be an exception if I want to climb to the next level", and on and on. When the same excuses emerge year after year, there is a question to be asked: **Who's running your life – your own deeply rooted sense of purpose or your external roles shaped by others?**

If you could connect the passion and purpose you distilled in the previous chapter to the select, strategic activities that would fulfill you in this current chapter of your life – what would those activities be? Remember, what counts is not the quantity of activities but the quality links among your emerging passions, sense of purpose, and strategic roles and activities.

Define Your Roles and Activities

Everybody has roles – things we do over and over, in certain settings – as a leader, volunteer, parent, partner and more. Adults have many roles in life.

You cannot live without meaningful roles in the world around you – in families, career, work organizations, friendship associations, civic and professional groups and communities. The problem is that over the years, many of our roles do not remain as meaningful and fulfilling as they used to be, while others grow to be more promising than ever. It is up to you to alter and retool your roles.

> *I looked on child rearing not only as a work of love and duty but as a profession that was fully as interesting and challenging as any honorable profession in the world, and one that demanded the best that I could bring to it.*
>
> — Rose Kennedy

Map Three

Map Three

Map 3, The Roles and Systems in our Lives, has six areas within which we devise activities for ourselves, or have them assigned to us: personal (self), family, couple, friends, work, and community.

1. The Personal (Self) Role – the care and feeding of you

More than a role, this is at the root of all we do and be in the world – the self, the core of our being, our centering mechanism, the driver of our passions and values. For now, though, we'll count it as a role insofar as the 'self' requires tending to as well.

The Role: This is our core that we must be connected to in order to live a meaningful life from the inside-out.

The Challenges: The roles in our lives are so demanding that you can lose track of your core 'self' and begin to exist as a collection of roles responding to whatever comes at us first – without the rudder of your values to guide the way – living a life of roles without soul.

The Activities:

- Intentional use of personal space areas at home and at work
- Care for the body through good nutrition and exercise
- Continual cultivation of the inner dialogue
- Personal time, alone
- Personal self-care and nurturing
- Personal spirituality in whatever form you choose
- Reading and learning that supports personal growth
- Management of priorities
- Budget and money management
- Other

In your journal, organize your personal activities for the next couple of years into three categories:

1. *Essential:* Those activities that are essential and necessary for you at this time in your life, whether you like them or not. In the next chapter of your life, how can you effectively maintain your essential personal activities?

2.*Fulfilling:* Those activities that are fulfilling for you at this time of your life – the ones you prefer and like the best. How can you increase your investment in your fulfilling personal activities?

3.*Unfulfilling:* Those activities that are unrewarding or even punishing at this time of your life. In the next chapter of your life, how can you eliminate or at least diminish your unfulfilling personal activities?

2. The Couple or Partner Role – the care and feeding of your primary relationship

We don't get much training in "coupling," yet this adult role often weaves through most of the others. It's here we share our most intimate concerns as lover, friend and advocate. This role isn't always active in our lives and it's not always a choice either. In today's world marriage is on a slight decline, divorce rates are high, alternative lifestyles are mainstream, and our aging populations are paving the way for communal living arrangements, solo living and remarriage as well. In the twenty-first century we are broadening the concept of the partnering role.

The Role: There is little that prepares us to be our best as a member of a dyad. Perhaps the model of our parents is the standard, most consistent mold we have to follow. Yet, without adequate skills and attention, this powerful role has the potential to bring us great joy or endless misery. More than any other role, this one requires a dance between individuation and togetherness, me and we, us in the world.

The Challenges: The challenges are endless because this is as "up close and personal" as it gets in life. How we learn to negotiate our differences, manage conflict, make decisions, care for one another and together navigate through all the other roles and systems in our lives – these are mighty challenges!

The Activities:

- Top of the list and early on in this role – enroll in workshops and classes focused on developing your relationship skills

And in the end, the love you take is equal to the love you make.

— The Beatles

- Create regular times for talking through the tough stuff
- Talk and touch regularly
- Share roles, tasks and fun
- Share projects and activities outside the home
- Engage in separate projects and activities outside the home
- Manage priorities
- Manage conflicts
- Create time for intimacy and sex
- Cultivate couple's friendships
- Interface with each other's work commitments
- Manage shared health needs
- Budget and manage money jointly and regularly
- Develop recreation and leisure activities
- Engage in adventure, learning and traveling together
- Other

In your journal, organize your couple/partner activities for the next two years into three categories:

1. *Essential:* Those activities that are essential and necessary for you at this time in your life, whether you like them or not. In the next chapter of your life, how can you effectively maintain your essential couple/partner activities?

2. *Fulfilling:* Those activities that are fulfilling for you at this time of your life – the ones you prefer and like the best. How can you increase your investment in your fulfilling couple/partner activities?

3. *Unfulfilling:* Those activities that are unrewarding or even punishing at this time of your life. In the next chapter of your life, how can you eliminate or at least diminish your unfulfilling couple/partner activities?

3. The Family Role – caring for children and parents

The activities that attend managing the family system network are complex and varied. Parenting alone is a very demanding role, requiring deep commitment, caring, leadership, time, and patience. Parenting activities change as children grow up. Many adults find themselves engaged in parenting 'nearly' adult children while simultaneously caring for their aging parents.

The Role: If this is a role you choose for your life, there is nothing as powerful or as transformative as the work of a parent. It tests our understanding of self every bit as much or more than the role of a couple or partner does this. Unlike any other role, it is 24/7 around the clock for almost a quarter of a century. By the time a child leaves home for college you've together invested nearly 7,500 days in your relationship, more heart than thought you had, and most likely you've experienced some tough challenges along the way as well. The role of parent inevitably brings us back to our own experience as a child and it offers us an opportunity to 'do it our way' this time around.

The Challenges: This is another role we 'fall into' without much preparation and certainly no classes or training in your schooling unless early childhood education was your specialty. This fact alone makes the role challenging and invigorating. The landscape changes with each year, the issues shift and the approaches must change as well. This role is inextricably wound up in the health of your couple/partner role because it is optimally a two person job raising kids. So the challenges are redoubled on this front. Challenges are even more daunting as a single parent and the workload twice as heavy.

To be nobody-but-yourself – in a world which is doing its best, night and day, to make you everybody else – means to fight the hardest battle which any human being can fight; and never stop fighting.

— e. e. cummings

The Activities:

- Top of the list is training, classes and workshops at every step of the way to support development of strong parenting skills
- Cooking and eating together
- Maintaining the home together
- Education of children
- Enjoying adventures and vacations
- Management of health needs
- Sports activities and hobbies
- Family friends
- Spiritual development, ethics and values
- Caring for parents
- Nurturing extended family
- At home learning, lessons, help

In your journal, organize your family activities for the next two years into three categories:

1. *Essential:* Those activities that are essential and necessary for you at this time in your life, whether you like them or not. In the next chapter of your life, how can you effectively maintain your essential family activities?

2. *Fulfilling:* Those activities that are fulfilling for you at this time of your life – the ones you prefer and like the best. How can you increase your investment in your fulfilling family activities?

3. *Unfulfilling:* Those activities that are unrewarding or even punishing at this time of your life. In the next chapter of your life, how can you eliminate or at least diminish your unfulfilling family activities?

4. The Friends Role – care and feeding of close friendships

Emerson said, "A friend may well be reckoned the masterpiece of nature." Aristotle talked of friends as important extensions of self, singer Bette Midler belts out the words "Oh... you've got to have friends, the feeling is oh so strong". Research bears out this message – we need friends to be healthy human beings in the world. Matter of fact, most research suggests we need at least a handful of close friends at all times in our lives in order to flourish. And we know from experience that you have to be a good friend in order to have the same in your life.

The Role: Friendship, meaningful long-term relationships we freely choose in our lives require commitment, dependability, a listening ear, and an ability to engage and be present for another in the good times and the bad.

The Challenges: Time and commitment are at the top of this list. When life gets busy it's harder to make the time for what can seem like 'optional' activities. Yet, sustaining long-term friendships is key to our wellbeing.

The daily pressures to act, to do, to decide, make it difficult to stop and think, to consider, and to examine your life goals, directions, and priorities – to find the best choices you have for managing your own world.

— Roy Menninger

The Activities:

- An evening outing, dinner, movies
- A long walk
- An at-a-distance telephone conversation
- Attending a sports event
- An annual golf or spa weekend
- A yoga class together
- A book group
- An adult education class
- Volunteer activities

In your journal, organize your friendship activities for the next two years into three categories:

1. *Essential:* Those activities that are essential and necessary for you at this time in your life, whether you like them or not. In the next chapter of your life, how can you effectively maintain your essential friendship activities?

2. *Fulfilling:* Those activities that are fulfilling for you at this time of your life – the ones you prefer and like the best. How can you increase your investment in your fulfilling friendship activities?

3. *Unfulfilling:* Those activities that are unrewarding or even punishing at this time of your life. In the next chapter of your life, how can you eliminate or at least diminish your unfulfilling friendship activities?

5. The Work Role – your job, career, or volunteer efforts to make a living and to find meaning

Most adults spend more time in their work activities than in any other area. In the western cultures this role continues to erode our ability to fully engage in other parts of our lives adequately. The Wall Street Journal recently noted that in 2007 a shocking 40% of Americans left 50% of their vacation time unused!

The Role: Our work roles vary at different times in our life. We work for many reasons and those reasons keep shifting over the years – to acquire a necessary level of financial security, to

We can never be really prepared for that which is wholly new. We have to adjust ourselves, and every radical adjustment is a crisis in self-esteem; we undergo a test, we have to prove ourselves. It needs inordinate self-confidence to face drastic change without inner trembling.

— Eric Hoffer

complete a final lap in our career, to be challenged and rewarded, to lead and make important contributions, and more.

The Challenges: Finding a balance point in the work role that allows you to engage fully in other important roles as well. Finding work that connects with your passion and becomes a most pleasurable part of your life.

The Activities:
- Commuting or not commuting
- Completing work assignments effectively
- Career advancement and coaching
- Weekend assignments
- Work friends
- Leadership
- Business travel
- Management
- Supervising others
- Leading an organization
- Getting results
- Necessary career step
- Retirement planning

Life means for us constantly to transform into light and flame all that we are or meet with.

— Friedrich Nietzsche

In your journal, organize your work activities for the next two years into three categories:

1. *Essential:* Those activities that are essential and necessary for you at this time in your life, whether you like them or not. In the next chapter of your life, how can you effectively maintain your essential work activities?

2. *Fulfilling:* Those activities that are fulfilling for you at this time of your life – the ones you prefer and like the best. How can you increase your investment in your fulfilling work activities?

3. *Unfulfilling:* Those activities that are unrewarding or even punishing at this time of your life. In the next chapter of your life, how can you eliminate or at least diminish your unfulfilling work activities?

6. Community and Volunteer Role – your involvement in community activities

None of us would have functional lives if it were not for a broad-based society that sustained sufficient order and meaning for our personal and family lives. At some point in the adult journey, most of us find some way to contribute back to the broader context of our world.

The Role: Our community and volunteer role diminishes and grows at different times along our journey and there's little doubt that our mature years are particularly ripe for use in this important role. Whether it be serving on boards, becoming politically active, making financial contributions or finding ways alone to make a difference – there are endless opportunities at all times in the adult journey.

The Challenges: Identifying and finding those causes that are aligned with your values takes a bit of research in every community. Making the commitment at a values level opens the door to saying 'yes'.

The Activities:

- Participation in community groups
- Membership in professional organizations
- Commitment to neighborhood
- Participation in social causes and political groups
- Volunteer activities in the community
- Participation on non-profit boards
- Awareness of the larger global community

In your journal, organize your community activities for the next two years into three categories:

1. *Essential:* Those activities that are essential and necessary for you at this time in your life, whether you like them or not. In the next chapter of your life, how can you effectively maintain your essential community and volunteer activities?

2. *Fulfilling:* Those activities that are fulfilling for you at this time of your life – the ones you prefer and like the best.

Our task must be to free ourselves from this prison by widening our circle of compassion to embrace all living creatures, and the whole of nature in its beauty.

— Albert Einstein

How can you increase your investment in your fulfilling community and volunteer activities?

3. *Unfulfilling:* Those activities that are unrewarding or even punishing at this time of your life. In the next chapter of your life, how can you eliminate or at least diminish your unfulfilling community and volunteer activities?

The sole purpose of life is to serve humanity.

— Leo Tolstoy

Example

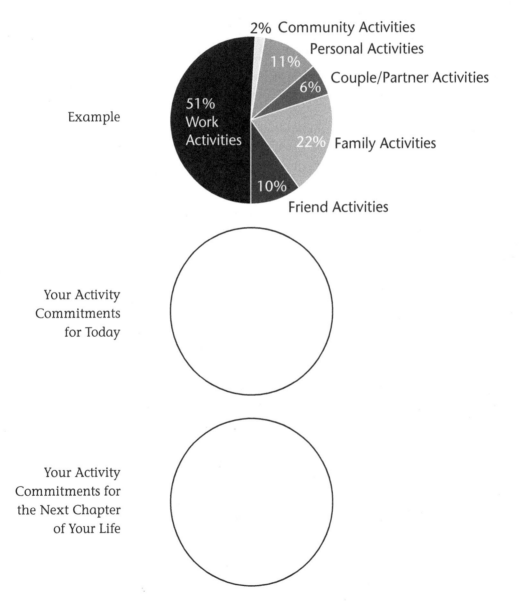

Your Activity Commitments for Today

Your Activity Commitments for the Next Chapter of Your Life

How Do You Balance Your Activities and Roles?

As adults we are often mightily challenged to manage and balance our evolving activities and roles. We can feel like we are drowning in the very activities we chose to swim in.

To achieve balance, become a master of spending your time where it matters most to you. That means making it a priority to find the necessary time to invest in your most essential and fulfilling activities while keeping your less fulfilling activities on the fringes.

To a large degree, who you are gets reflected in the way you spend your time, and the roles within which you spend your time shape your being, your outlook and your concerns. The following experiment asks you to do two things: first, to discover how much time you are now giving to each of your roles; and second, to calculate how much time you want to give to each of those roles during the next chapter of your life.

Instructions: *Using the six areas of activities just reviewed – personal, couple or partner, family, friends, community, and work – conduct an inventory of how much time you currently spend in each area, and how much time you want to spend in those same areas during the next few years. Include weekday and weekend events, excluding sleep. Assume you are awake and involved for **100 hours per week**.*

1. First make a list of how you spend your time in the current chapter of your life, using the formula of 100 hours of waking time per week to spread among your current activities and roles. Use percentages and be sure they add up to 100%.

2. Then make a second list for how you want to invest your time in preferred activities and roles in the forthcoming chapter of your life.

Think not of yourselves, O Chiefs, nor of your own generation. Think of continuing generations of our families, think of our grandchildren and of those yet unborn, whose faces are coming from beneath the ground.

— Iroquois Chief

3. When you are done with these approximate mathematical measures of your commitments, transfer them to the two circles (pies), assuming that each circle equals 100 hours and each quarter circle is equivalent to 25 hours. Let each percentage become a slice of pie within a circle.

Your Commitments in The Next Chapter of Your Life

Adult change is every bit as social as it is personal. Too often adults think they can individually change their lives, irrespective of the roles and activities they have. **In fact, change is more of a dialogue between you and all the people and parts of your current life context than anything else.** Gradually, you can increase or diminish your investment in any activity or role, but any change will involve some shift in another role. You trade off one for another, reducing time commitments in one area while increasing time commitments in another. Passionate, on-purpose adults know how to honor, manipulate, shape, respect, and accept the complex time commitments that their lives represent. Are you ready to do that in your next chapter?

Chapter Seven

Map 4

The Grand Adventure
The Adult Journey

Human beings have always employed an enormous variety of clever devices for running away from themselves.... We can keep ourselves so busy, fill our lives with so many diversions, stuff our heads with so much knowledge, involve ourselves with so many people, and cover so much ground that we never have time to probe the fearful and wonderful world within.... By middle life, most of us are accomplished fugitives from ourselves. — John Gardner

---

The Grand Adventure
The Adult Journey

Map 4 describes the contours of our adult journey, highlighting common themes over time, drawing our attention to the multitude of 'unexpected visitors' along the road, and always measuring tomorrow by yesterday's familiar scenes. The beginning of each new decade (30, 40, 50, etc) seems to naturally accentuate where we've been and invite a certain amount of self examination about where we are going and how it's all coming together. The passing of each successive decade reminds us the journey is finite and this growing awareness often serves to intensify purposeful living.

In spite of the shifting tide of our twenty-first century demographics, we still tend to make "young" the ideal and the norm. Yet more and more of us imagine we can deepen the human journey as we get older, and create richly textured lives well into our eighties!

The challenge of this chapter highlighting the adult journey is to convey how our lives get richer, more complex and more resilient, even as our bodies slow down and our physical appearance shifts from taunt and muscular to soft and relaxed.

Each new chapter in our adult journey can feel like a distinctly different time, woven into the old familiar and guided by shifting concerns and opportunities of the time. Our chapters tend to consolidate around certain themes and in the twenty-first century these themes are more varied than every before.

Each trip around the never-ending cycle of change and renewal taps different passions and values that lead you to a new sense of equilibrium on the inside and outside, rebalancing your perception of essential roles and priorities – providing you with a new élan for life. This cycle is the foundation for our creative growth throughout life's journey.

The true measure of your journey through the adult years is not your age, for life is not about staying young forever. The profound and tangible measure of one's life is found in your capacity to remain fully engaged in an ever changing journey.

I was thinking again of age and of what in each season seems just out of reach, just beyond what is in front of us, a kind of ghost of what we see, to which we offer up our days.

— W. S. Merwin

People travel to wonder at the height of mountains, and they pass by themselves without wondering.

— St. Augustine

Each trip around the cycle you deepen your life experience, examine new realms of growth, and put and end to some worn out ways. True maturity is based upon what you have learned and become along the way, not a reflection of your chronological age.

Life is a series of trade-offs, with some parts of you becoming more present and competent while others fall away. At all times what is true is that some aspects of your life lose importance during the journey while other dimensions gain in relevance. Getting older is not about getting worse or better; it's about getting different. The more you engage in life at each step along the path, the more interesting the journey; and as physical strengths and attributes diminish over time, our inner, spiritual strengths seem to naturally grow. Engagement is the key, the thirst, and the challenge for us.

We each change in different ways at different times in our lives for many reasons. Sometimes change comes in the form of an external event that causes a major and sudden shock to all systems in our life – the most dramatic of these is death and disease. Oddly enough, we are almost universally surprised when this happens to us, living with a hope that big endings or shocking surprises are reserved only for 'others'. On other occasions, change percolates over time, from the inside-out – perhaps it's the brewing desire to leave your career and start a business of your own or the knowing that your relationship is no longer feeding either of you and it's time to find a graceful way to say goodbye.

Both the external and inside-out changes turn our lives upside down and naturally draw us to the part of the cycle where we grieve, we rail, we let go and we slowly shed an old layer of our 'self' and step into a new chapter. Pay attention to your issues, priorities, concerns and passions at these change times when you begin to formulate the next chapter of your life. There are no firm rules to follow, no predictable stages to enter, no reason to conform to age stereotypes. Just be deliberate as you plan your life and live it, your way, no matter where you are on the adult journey.

The more you know about the range of options in front of you, the less you fear them, deny them, or fail to thrive on them. The more you know about the patterns and discernible features of the journey, the easier it will be to find your way.

Frederic Hudson's outline of the key concepts of the life cycle (reference *The Adult Years* pages 129-133), is a good starting point for understanding the terrain. His studies reveal eleven key concepts including:

1. **The childhood years shape, limit, and enrich the adult years.** We've long known that our early years are powerfully formative. Spanning the history of developmental psychology, the work of Freud, Jung, Klein, Erickson, Gilligan and many others have taught us this. What does this translate into as adults – our beliefs, our defensive positions, our stance about life itself, our sense of self, our sense of safety in the world, our disposition for risk and challenge. Nothing short of fundamental to who we are and how we travel the adult journey.

2. **Healthy adults adapt and grow throughout the adult years.** We are continually adapting to changes we've intentionally crafted from the inside-out, as well as those that are foisted upon us from the world around us. Our ability to integrate these changes into our lives and take a trip around the cycle in order to shed old parts of the self and re-craft new dimensions – this is what makes for healthy 'adulting'.

3. **The adult years are a process of ongoing change and continuity.** At one time in history experts believed most development took place in the childhood and adolescent years. Now we know that's just not so. We are continually developing and changing if we are open to the journey. Stagnation is what happens to those who choose to continually live in the past without full engagement in their life today.

4. **Social status is a major determinant of adult development issues and directions.** There's no escaping the reality that education creates possibilities and options for our future. It's also true that 'socio-economic' factors of social status and financial health are either stepping stones or obstacles in the adult journey. Maslow's well-known hierarchy of

Too many young people are growing up today unable to handle life in hard places, without hope, without adequate attention, and without steady internal compasses to navigate the morally polluted seas they must face on the journey to adulthood.

— Marion Wright Edelman

needs is the best explanation of how this works – if our focus is on the survival level of food and shelter, we aren't likely to have an advantage of other challenges.

I have a sense of urgency about accomplishing my work – a sense of limited time – but there is no frenzy in it, no hanging cloud raining dark thoughts of approaching infirmities or death.

— Larry L. King

5. **There are dramatic differences between the styles and priorities of men and women during the adult life cycle.** Timing, preferences, choices and styles vary widely between genders, and some of this is built into the larger culture and some specific to gender preferences.

6. **Careers and work environments have considerable impact on our adult lives.** Most of us spend many hours of each day in a work setting and the nature of our work, the quality of our peer associations, the quest and vision of the organizations we support all have a significant impact on our lives. There is potential for a very positive upside and a serious downside in this – so choosing one's work, one's setting and to a large extent, one's associates – these are important places for personal intentionality.

7. **Adults in midlife and elderhood often become preoccupied with their mortal limits, death and time left to live.** This is not all a negative thing! Developmentalist Bernice Neugarten noted a shift in the way we measure time that seems to arrive about midway through life's journey, when *time left* becomes more important than *time until*. This powerful shift turns up the dial on what's most important for us to be doing, driving us closer to what we are passionate about and shedding what's no longer compelling in our lives.

8. **Adults in midlife often experience an increase in individuation and introspection.** The inner journey is simply more appealing as we grow older. We are interested in a deeper connection with ourselves and the larger world.

9. **During the adult years, leisure – or, more fundamentally, play – takes on a new meaning, as a vehicle for living rather than as a vacation from working.** In our early adult years we work and then play, or work to play; as we grow older we begin to see the wisdom of incorporating play and leisure into our daily routines.

10. **A major trend in midlife is the pursuit of personal integrity.** Most of us have made some compromises along the way and we justify them in the context of the demands we juggle, but as we grow older we seem to want to 'right the course' and live as close to our personal beliefs as possible.

11. **In midlife, adults frequently become more invested in leadership roles and social contribution.** This is a natural progression for most of us. We've acquired skills, we've developed leadership capacities, we are at a time in our lives when contribution ought to be on the forefront – it's important for us, it's important for the world we have grown up in.

The purpose of life is a life of purpose.

— Marvin Banasky

The work of key developmentalists points to a general shift in perspective occurring somewhere midway along the journey. This shift has been popularized by the term 'midlife crisis', but in fact, it seems to exist for most of us and marks a turning point in our lives. Jung wrote extensively about this phenomenon, accentuating the deep shifts in our perspective that happen along life's journey. He believed we experienced a major reshaping of our stance and our approach to life somewhere about midway through the adult years. The first half seems largely to focus on what he terms the 'heroic' – reaching new heights in our work, striving for achievements, competing for the best, succeeding in relationships, collecting the important cultural possessions and more. Then, sometime in the middle years our focus begins to shift from the outer journey to the deeper inner pilgrimage. We are less concerned about the external strivings, the recognition from the world, and more attuned to our inner dialogue, our emerging and shifting passions, our sense of something beyond ourselves.

Traditionally the adult journey has been mapped using ages and stages as the anchor for understanding what we can expect, how we ought to behave and travel along the journey. This linear approach made a lot of sense when life was more stable and predictable than today and social norms were more restrictive relative to what and how we led our lives along the journey.

> *The least of things with a meaning is worth more in life than the greatest of things without it.*
>
> — Carl Jung

Today, our adult years span almost twice the years of Jung's time, and our crisis points and chapters are many. There is growing literature that a 'quarter life crisis' exists for us in our twenties and early thirties given the abundance of new choices available and a preponderance of old maps that no longer fit today's journey. Social prescriptions and constraints no longer pressure us to marry, have children, develop long term careers, and move in a lock-step fashion. Instead, we have permission to remain single, wait to develop a career path, choose to be childless, and largely step out of our parent's social mores. We've also been largely liberated from yesterday's ideas about our elder years. When our life span was shorter and the social constructs were stronger, we 'retired' at 60 or 65. If we were lucky we moved into a retirement community with like-minded folks where we finally had a chance to relax, tend the golf game, socialize and enjoy the final stretch.

Today's picture is dramatically different with health and longevity on the increase, savings on the decrease, and 'retirement' a concept we are outgrowing. So the reinvention of the 60's decade and beyond creates yet another crisis of sorts, as we shift into our later years with new choices, new tasks and old formulas that don't work so well anymore.

Where are the guides for understanding the landscape of this expansive period of time likely to range from the early twenties until our nineties or more? Does the scaffolding of the past work in our changing world? Yes and no – there is truth to be found in our past formulations and yet it's more complex today, and we need some new game plans to prosper in today's world.

Developmentalists until recently conceived of a decade by decade representation for understanding the adult landscape. The popular 'decade' approach made sense, it was generally true and it offered signposts to us for the path ahead. While there is still value in the 'decade' approach, it's far more complicated today.

The Decades Perspective

Let's review what remains useful about the decades by noticing the broad themes. We long characterized the twenties as a time for starting just about everything from leaving home to starting college; from college to career; marriage and then family; home and all of the demands these roles entail. The twenties remains a time for leaving home, for forging one's identity, for experimenting, learning, working, enjoying friends and trying out intimate relationships, but the terrain is not as predictable, the sequence varies widely, and the options are more diverse than ever.

The thirties is still likely to be our strongest launch pad into the career trajectory, and more and more this is the time when couples who choose to have children take on this new role – often stretching the 'maternal clock' into the later thirties and well into the forties as well.

The forties and fifties tend to be the peak of the balancing act of various roles – from professional or work to parent, to marital or life partner to community or civic volunteer – these are typically the most demanding years. The fifties are now touted by Gail Sheehy and others as some of the happiest years on the adult journey, bringing with it a time of satisfaction, economic stability, perspective and growing wisdom as well.

The shift into the sixties is new territory in the twenty-first century, opening up the possibility of what Boomer writer Mary Furlong terms a 'bonus round' of another 20 to 30 healthy years and essentially a new stage of life.

While the decades still contain broad markers for the developmental journey, in many ways we've released ourselves from the social molds of the past and we can now decide from the 'inside out' just what it is we want to do and when we want to do it.

Take the task of parenthood – not so long ago this was seen as a development 'goal' of the twenties decade. Today, those who choose to have children begin families in their twenties, thirties, forties and, in some cases, fifties. What's more, the decision whether to have children is a real and acceptable choice today leaving an increasing number of adults childless by choice.

Career pathways have changed as well. Not so long ago the prescribed approach to career was an immediate transition from college into the first career position

*Midway life's journey
I was made aware
That I had strayed
into a dark forest,
And the right path
Appeared not
anymore.*

— Dante

and onward and upward! Today's college graduates are much more likely to experiment, travel, explore the possibilities and generally leave themselves plenty of time and space to craft their first life chapter just as they would like it.

> *It is better to err on the side of daring than the side of caution.*
>
> — Alvin Toffler

In short, a decade and age specific approach to understanding the adult journey is no longer the 'essential guide' – it's simply more complex. Decades, ages, and stages continue to provide us with some markers and general trends that are useful, but this approach is too simplistic in a world that is less prescriptive than the twentieth century.

So today, we offer you a mosaic of the general patterns of the new adult terrain that includes broader groupings and phases with far wider variations. The three phases include: The First Launch, The Second Launch and The Third Launch.

What follows is a handful of narratives that highlight some of the nuances and challenges to life found in each of these three broad phases.

Map Four

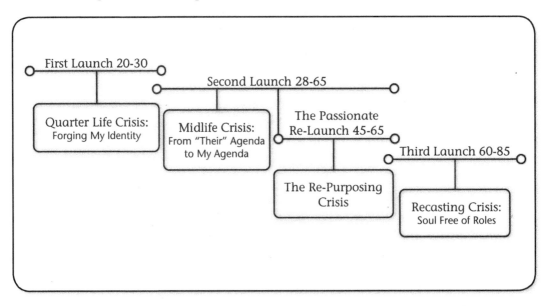

First Launch – Forging my Identity

For all of us, the First Launch marks our initial foray into adult life. It's tenuous, it's exciting, it's electrifying to be 'out of the house' and it's disquieting – all at the same time. If we are lucky, we spend a few years in college and gain some knowledge and skills that send us out into the world with a bit of confidence about the steps ahead. For some this path is about acquiring a technical skill set and for others the path is a broader field of study.

In today's world, this whole phase seems to roll out at a slower pace than it did in the past. First, the burden of finances – college expenses as well as living expenses in many parts of the world are so exorbitant that it's simply harder to get a firm footing at the outset. More young adults in their twenties return home following college to live and work while getting some leverage for the next phase of life. More young adults create tribes of their own choosing wherein there is shared living, cooking, and decision-making around all of life's choices. Possibilities seem endless at this time of life while commitments are generally fewer than at any other time on the adult journey.

Notes from a 21 year old...

OK, it's happened – I've finished college. I keep reminding myself this is what I've been waiting for, this is what I've been dying to do – say goodbye to college life, exams, dorms, complicated living arrangements and all that goes with the 'college experience'.

And yet, the voices screaming in my head saying "OK, Teri, what are you going to do now? What about your plan to visit the career center regularly, to check out job possibilities? Where is my perfect resume? Just what is a Communications Major supposed to do after college? And, by the way, how am I supposed to make these decisions all alone? OK, maybe I'm not alone, but I can't rely on my parents to help me figure this one out and most of my friends seems as confused as I, so just where do I turn?

I keep coming back to two choices: stay here in Chicago where I know I can at least keep my waitress job while I figure out this whole complicated mess or take a big leap, apply for jobs anywhere and start a whole new life in a place I've never been, with people I've never met, doing things I've probably never done! Can I spell P-A-R-A-L-Z-Y-E-D! My roomies keep telling me I ought to consider one more choice: move back to my parents for a year or two – to buy some time, save some money and slowly figure out my next step.

Our twenty-one year old captures the heart of the new challenges found in the early launch into adulthood. While it's great to have choices without the old social formulas, these seemingly endless choices also create plenty of growing pains. The early twenties is all about forging one's identity and by the time we've added a few years of experimenting with what's interesting and what's possible, we also begin to gain some clarity about who we are. The following narrative captures the dramatic shifts that occur during this vast distance from the early twenties to the later ones.

Notes from a 26 year old...

Well, it's been almost four years since I finished my undergraduate studies and I'm sitting here applying to graduate schools. I'm still not thoroughly convinced this is the right choice for me, but I guess I'm ready to try it on. I've spent the last three years traveling the world. My first year was funded by a fellowship and I lived in three different parts of China. It has been an awesome experience and at times a lonely one as well. I went to Shanghai first and left behind a relationship that was as close to perfect as I imagine they come. The first few months were a combination of exhilarating on the work and language front and frustrating and sad on the relationship side --- we kept trying to figure out what to do, how to talk about this time, how to be with so many miles between us, and the whole thing caused both of us a lot of anguish. Even now, as I look back on our decisions, I'm not sure they were the right ones, I'm not sure I won't always have some regret about leaving behind a great, great woman. But I did and she did, and in the meantime, I slowly began tackling Mandarin, and learning about some parts of the Chinese culture.

I unexpectedly stumbled into some work (I was broke and needed money more than anything) at a radio station – the British version of NPR, and that led to another two years of work – first in Hong Kong and finally in the countryside. I had absolutely no knowledge of radio nor any interest in it until I read an online job ad. What began as a lark has opened up a whole new world to me. I've always had decent writing skills and a strong interest in 'the person on the street', and it somehow all fit together. I have spent two years doing special interest stories and weaving them into something that I've used on a weekly show. It's tempting to continue on this path, but I still have this gnawing hope that I can influence some change in the world, and I don't think I'm going to do it sitting in the middle of rural

China -- so here I am applying for graduate school, back in the U.S., hoping to connect with some old college friends, feeling a little lonely at this stage, trying to figure out whether I'm way behind my peers, a little ahead, or completely off track with everything from career to relationships.

Whatever the path, this is a time of maximum freedom and minimal roles and responsibilities. If you are lucky, the only person you are responsible for and to is YOU. And paradoxically, that is the biggest challenge for most of us – it's a daunting proposition to consider being alone in the world with endless choices and for the most part, no one to satisfy but oneself.

This is the work of this phase – forging our identity through exploration, work experiments, travel, relationships, and risk-taking – and the good news is that those entering their twenties are getting smarter about taking their time in this phase. We used to gasp if a twenty-three year old wasn't on a career track, embedded in the line of work they'd chosen soon after they entered college at age 18. How absurd of us to think we know much of anything about what we want in the adult journey at age 18! It takes time, experience, and experimenting to figure out even some of this puzzle and that's what twenty-something's are teaching us today.

The distance from 22 to 28 is a long road, and if you've engaged in enough 'testing of the waters' through jobs, travel, getting to know yourself, experimenting with the endless possibilities life has to offer through quality experiences, making good choices that allowed for growth – you arrive at the portal to your late twenties firmly grounded in an identity you've forged through your choices, your risks, your flat-out failures and your commitments.

So what's the Quarter Life Crisis – we never used to talk about a crisis at this early stage in the adult journey, so why now? Let's face it, until recently we relied on a fairly rigid social mold for this phase of life – finishing college, finding a good career path, a mate, settling down, perhaps starting a family, finding the right home. This sequential, lock-step formula is no longer dominant in today's world of different paths to choose. The Quarter Life Crises is embedded in a new suite of multiple choices.

Twenty-something's today have more permission than ever before to sculpt and shape a path of their own choosing. They may explore different jobs in several companies before choosing a more lasting position because their loyalties are to their own skill sets and competencies; they may purchase a starter home knowing they can sell it and move up to a larger home in a few years, or move to another city; they may travel to countries in the far corners of the world; they may take on challenges and join groups to solve social problems that affect global communities. And they may be engaged in all of these activities simultaneously. 'Testing the waters' and exploring life's possibilities may lead to self-directed twenty-something's moving into their middle years with a strong sense of direction.

Blueprint for a Successful First Launch

- **Get to Know Yourself First.** This is probably the biggest challenge and the most often daunting, but it's important, it's the right time, and it takes time. Get to know yourself before you commit to a career path or a graduate degree. Get to know yourself before you get wrapped up in a relationship – you'll have a much better sense of what you want in someone else, of what works in someone else and what will serve you both over the long haul. Taking new risks is a great way to get acquainted with yourself at this stage in life!

- **Stay Away from Too Many Commitments Too Soon.** This is a trap that's easy to fall into. After all, an anchor or two can make the future a little easier to tackle. So rely on good friends, family, and make close connections that don't require a lifelong commitment. And here's why: our choices at age 22 aren't likely to be the same ones we would make at age 28 for many reasons.

- **Fear and Excitement are Partners!** The toughest challenge at this stage in life is the sheer number of choices in front of us; and yet, this is also what makes it so exciting. All options are OPEN, all possibilities are worth consideration, all roads are yet to be traveled and in a sense, all learning is just now beginning. The upside is possibilities galore and the downside is getting overwhelmed and making ourselves much smaller than we need to be. Taking the first job that

Life is a mystery – unfold it.
Life is struggle – face it.
Life is beauty – praise it.
Life is a puzzle – solve it.

— Anonymous

comes along, staying too close to old routines, hanging on to our college buddies and not venturing out too far. When fear comes knocking and threatens to shrink your dreams, notice that excitement shows up as well. If not now, when?

- **Travel, Explore, Intern, Find a fellowship, Treat life as a temporary experiment for a few years.** There are few times in life when you are this free to literally 'try on' various life paths, locations, relationships, work settings and fields of study. Sometimes we grab a hold of some security in order to avoid the sheer sense of fear we have when looking out at the wide open field. Plan ahead, look into possibilities that expand your horizons.

- **Manage Your Money. Money management is a big part of this phase.** Learning to make it, spend it, save it and pay your way is a bigger task than ever in today's marketplace. Many, many graduates of colleges enter the world with a load of debt on their backs. Live within your means, spend only what you earn and save a little at all times. Don't allow your dreams to be derailed by your spending habits.

- **Experiment with Career Options.** Don't lock yourself in to a particular career path too early. Allow time for experimenting, following a wild dream or two, testing possibilities that you are truly passionate about. Risk, ask for help, network, dare to be bold. This time in life is meant for exploration – give yourself permission to 'try on' a variety of options before settling in for a longer journey. Try internships early on, find a fellowship, part-time summer jobs, sign on for early career jobs with a short view instead of a long term commitment, seek out mentors and experts and ask their advice, network and leverage your options.

- **Learn how to Sustain Loving Relationships.** Learning how to nurture deep and lasting friendships and intimate relationships will serve you for a lifetime, and the learning is often not easy. Most of us bring what we have learned from our families about how to nurture important relationships and this inevitably creates some challenges. Know this is so, trust that it takes you and another to create problems and solutions. Use this time in life to build your capacity in this important part of life. Seek resources and accept

*Life is opportunity – take it.
Life is sorrowful – experience it.
Life is a song – sing it.
Life is a goal – achieve it.
Life is a mission – fulfill it.*

— Anonymous

responsibility for your shortcomings and your strengths as a good friend and partner. Try reading, finding workshops focused on this topic, seek out a counselor or therapist in tough times.

- **Deepen Clarity about Your Values.** This is an evolving process and it requires developing an inner dialogue. For some this comes easily and for others it's quite a foreign concept. Spend some time alone and let your feelings bubble up. You'll start to notice what feels right and what doesn't. Try journaling, regular time alone, a meditation practice, reading the ideas of the latest thinkers in this domain – Po Bronson, Christine Hassler, Marcos Salazar, Alexandra Robbins and Abby Wilner.

> *The broad concept of middle age is starting later and lasting longer – and looking better than ever before. Contrary to conventional wisdom, many people find that the 50s is actually a period of reduced stress and anxiety.*
>
> — Melinda Beck

Second Launch: From 'Their Agenda to Mine' – The Midlife Crisis

The Second Launch spans a long period of time in the middle of life with two crisis points that seem inevitable for most of us. If you heed the call each time, you unleash a renewed and deepened sense of passion. The first turning point is early in this journey and marks the transition from the agenda of others to our own sense of what's most important. The second comes later in the journey – a crisis of repurposing that invites renewal and re-engagement if we are open to the journey, or stagnation if we refuse. Here are two narratives illustrating both of these crisis points:

Notes from a nearly 40 year old...

Well, it's now a year until my 40th birthday and I am moving through life at a faster pace than I ever imagined. I've got plenty to feel great about – not the least of which is my earning power. I never dreamed I would own the home I'm living in, travel to great new places on vacation, have a loving husband who puts up with my work schedule and a career path that looks brighter with each new year. So why do I have this growing turmoil inside, this trace of agitation that leaves me always feeling a little on edge?

I guess that in spite of feeling proud of my accomplishments and my outward signs of success – home, car, art collection and more, I begin to wonder ... you know, the trite phrase 'Is this all there is?".

I mean, I'm gone from my home and my husband over 50% of the year, I seldom have time to enjoy most of the 'things' I've collected as signs of my success. What's even more troubling, I find it hard to slow down. It's as though I have a voice in my head whispering to me 'come on, Jill, you can take it to the next level, there is more you can do, you've got more to accomplish – bring home another 'A' – and I'm haunted by that voice. Is it me? Am I running my life or is this a remote operation and I'm really being driven by old scripts and tapes passed on from my childhood?

What exactly would I change if I didn't carry those voices with me? How would I be living? -- now that's a good question! So, yes, I feel like the '40' marker is bringing with it a midlife crisis of sorts and I've got to get reacquainted with myself, figure out what's most important now that I'm certain I can do just about anything I want to.

Jill's story captures the essence of the early phase of the middle journey. For a long time it has been about climbing the mountain, feeling great about the ascent and fully immersed in all of the nuances – the jackknives, sheer cliffs, the shortness of breath and more; about all that's been collected on the way up – the mementos, the special stones, the acknowledgements, the applause, the attention, the accomplishments and finally the summit. For most of us, the summit is always a surprise, a view we didn't quite expect – most of us we look around and find it's not quite as sweet as we had imagined. At the top we become conscious that the challenges on the climb were more engaging, more fun than the view from atop. So it's here, at the top, we ask ourselves that all-important question: Was this worth the climb? Was this my idea? Is this what I really want to be doing? Is this somebody else's agenda? And if I constructed my own agenda, what exactly would I put on it?

This is the crossroads Jill finds herself standing at, and it is that critical time we ask ourselves the salient question: Who is running my life? Who's driving my agenda? Which scripts do I want to shed at this fork in the road and which do I keep; in other words, My Agenda, not yours anymore!

> *There is a special quality of life-power available only to those seasoned by struggles of four or more decades. The life-power of this stage can be especially profound.*
>
> — Robert Lifton

Blueprint for the Perfect Second Launch

---

*Life is too short to
be small.*

— Benjamin Disraeli

- **Notice when it arrives, don't dismiss it!** When doubt comes knocking at the door and you begin to notice some flaws in the course you are on, don't brush the doubt aside – it's part of the journey and it's signaling a time to shed others' dreams for your life and fully claim this one and only life as your own!

- **Build yourself a new Board of Advisors – Take time to identify the voices, the scripts, the messages** that continue to drive your agenda and motivate your next steps. These voices helped you reach this summit – now it's time to say thank you and become more discerning about the voices of the next chapter.

- **Talk with friends on this journey.** You may feel like you are the only one asking these questions, but chances are good that you have plenty of company. So, open the dialogue, find some good friends who are willing to engage in the same conversation you are having with yourself. Talking aloud gives us perspective and valuable input.

- **Grant yourself a 'Time Out'** – OK, this probably seems impossible to imagine, but it's just what is needed in order to gain some perspective. You don't have to shut down your life or the office in order to take some time out (although that's a great idea, too!) Maybe you figure out how to take a little time on a weekly basis, or a half day a month – just enough to press the 'pause' button and engage in some self examination.

- **Build an Inner Conversation.** You've been engaged in 'outer' work of accomplishing, doing, and becoming. Step back and consciously cultivate an inner conversation with yourself.

Second Launch Part II: Passionate Re-Launch – The Repurposing Crisis

The next crisis point in this Second Launch is easy to miss. At this middle stage in life, we are deeply embedded in so many relationships, commitments and work engagements. When we begin to sense a waning of the 'fire', a lessening of passion for all we are engaged in, it's often feels easier to just keep doing what you've been doing. Most of us don't want to 'rock the boat' too much at this juncture – we have a whole lot at stake at work and at home, in the economic realms and more. And yet it's almost inevitable that we arrive at a time when what we've been doing loses its appeal, when life doesn't have quite the shimmer we recall from the past.

I was in a phone conversation the other day with Robert, a colleague I've known for several years. A bright, talented leader starting the big 50 countdown. We were talking about how we keep the 'fire' alive in the fifties, and together we mused about how tempting it is to keep doing what we've always done at this stage in life because we are good at it, we are handsomely rewarded for it – and frankly we are in our comfort zone. Yet, the price is often the loss of 'the fire', the passion, that sense of newness that comes from traveling in unknown territory. As our conversation continued, my friend let down his guard a bit and said: *You know, when people ask me about my work these days, I respond with my pat answer 'I love my work, it's right in my sweet spot and I believe I'm making an important difference' – yet the reality is so far from this; truth is, I'm bored most of the time. I've done this, I know the terrain, the challenges aren't there anymore and for some reason, it's even hard to admit this to myself. After all, what's my option – to open Pandora's box?*

Another good friend, Janet, is at the mid-fifties mark. She started out as a journalism major in her undergraduate years, meandered into the world of I.T., I think in part because several years of summer admin work in an I.T. business in her college days stirred an interest in the field. By the time she was in her thirties she was fully engaged in more roles than most of us can manage – superbly parenting several children, managing multiple teams, finding time for her writing, finally publishing a mystery book – and thoroughly engaged in all parts of the journey. Slowly, she lost her passion for her work, and continued to 'give voice' to her writing in smaller projects – and I think her most satisfying work and love has been raising a family, managing the chaotic strivings and schedules of her great kids, encouraging them through the good times and the more challenging ones, and creating a sense of family at each step in the journey. Now, the kids are gone, the house is mostly

It's the heart afraid of breaking that never learns to dance. It's the dream afraid of waking that never takes the chance…. And the soul afraid of dying that never learns to live.

— Bette Midler
(*The Rose*)

quiet, and she could surely sit back, relax and feel good about all she's accomplished; and yet, there is a restlessness, a yearning for more, for uncharted territories and new challenges.

Notes from Janet at 55...

There are so many things that are just right about this time in life. I've long since given up the ghost of living someone else's agenda or plan; I have an awareness of great pleasure that the big race is over and the thrill of the climb is not it for me anymore. I guess I have a sense I have mostly arrived at the summit I had in mind and frankly, I don't need those external sources of confirmation much anymore! And there's no denying it, while there are bittersweet parts of the empty nest, it's also been just the right time in my life to have a new sense of spaciousness and quiet, an end to the late nights and empty fridge!

So what's the rub? Well it's this: I've done much of what I'd hoped to accomplish and many of the items on the list on my desk are 'slam dunks' – been there, done that sort of stuff. I just don't get the same WOW from much of what I do in my daily life – and maybe this is all part of getting a little older, I just don't know.

And then, there's my marriage – I love this guy I've been with for almost thirty years, we've been through plenty of ups and downs and now we pride ourselves in having 'perspective' – it's just that I've begun to worry that this word is synonymous with boring!

Here's what I ponder in my mind these days: Where has the passion gone? Is it my age? Does something need to change? I'm not ready or economically prepared to stop working, I don't plan to give up my husband and try a newer variety, I'm not one of those women who goes on a vacation alone and never returns home; but there's got to be a way to tap some new passion!

There are many such stories - the nuances are complex and varied, and yet, it seems that more often than not we arrive at this stage in life, this crisis of sorts, at some time during our fifties decade. We dub it "The Repurposing Crisis" – that space and time where we just don't feel the 'fire' in the same way anymore and we aren't ready to sit back and relax on the porch! We want more, we want different, we want a more compelling sense of purpose in the world. We know we're capable of creating something new – after all, we have a long history of accomplishments and achievements; and yet, we don't want to 'upset the apple cart' and give up the creature comforts we've worked so hard to create. This is the dilemma of this time in life – The Repurposing Crisis. If we listen to our restlessness and attend to our vague yearnings long enough, we'll open the door to experimenting in new territories. Experiences prove we can uncover some surprises, some sources of new energy and 'élan vital' if we are patient and stay on the journey even when it's tempting to take the easier path. James Hollis writes "The repurposing crisis offers us a chance to re-awaken all that matters, to re-assess what's most important at this crucial crossroads."

Blueprint for a Passionate Re-Launch

- The time is now for experiments. Don't just sit and look backward! It's time to pose that well-used question: "When was the last time you did something for the first time?" Experiment, try on some new adventures, a new language, an art form, a travel experience, a shift in career tracks or positions, downsize your house, redecorate your home to reflect you at this time in life.

- The time is now for clearing the clutter. You've had a lot of time to gather relationships, possessions, habits, ways of being. Lighten the load by consciously taking inventory of what matters and what is fast becoming clutter.

- The ticking clock is getting louder. If you are working, figure out how much longer you are going to need to and want to continue working at your current pace. Get specific, do the numbers, be realistic. Once you've landed on this number, notice how this sits with you, how it reframes your future, your possibilities and the limits as well.

- The unlived dreams are calling. Maybe it's time to reconnect with your past and notice those 'roads not traveled', those unlived dreams you once pondered. Do some journaling and see if you can slowly begin to construct a list of unlived dreams.

- Go somewhere new, all alone. Yes, find a spot you've always wanted to visit and schedule a trip alone – no family, no friends, just you! Spend as long as you can manage to slip away – a week, a month or more. Write, walk, sleep, and read. Notice what begins to surface for you, what you recall about past passions, what you have energy for on the horizon.

> *The first half of life is about compulsions; the second half is about choice.*
>
> — Shoshanna Zuboff

Third Launch: The Recasting Crisis

Somewhere in the distance between 60 and 70 we begin to look at life from a new vantage point. We feel the pressure of time in new ways and the 'Recasting Crisis' invites us to engage in some deep soul-searching around what's most important at this stage in life. The terrain is distinctly different than the well-traveled roads we've known so well. Work is no longer the strong, driving force and centerpiece in our life. We notice our final chapter is closer at hand. We long to leave a mark, create a lasting legacy, and carefully evaluate how we want to spend this stage in the journey. This challenge is the gift of being fully awake and engaged – and we have a powerful convergence of meaning and gratitude emerging. We consolidate and get comfortable with old inner conflicts and irrational ideas, we gain a newfound perspective. We quite simply have access to a sense of gratitude that hasn't existed in this way before.

This is no time to loosen the grip – in fact, there is no time more important than this stage to harvest the work of past phases, enjoy the fruits of your learning and your deep pool of experience and perspective. This is the chapter of life that marks the end of the middle and remains a far distance from the end. Some demographers say we are the recipients of a 30 year bonus round we never planned on – three decades representing a staggering series of possibilities and perils. We've developed medical solutions to problems that shortened our lifespan in the past, we've simultaneously increased our health and wellness practices, and the average lifespan of today's adult in a developed part of the world keeps creeping up toward well into the 80's and 90's.

This is a fundamental shift that shakes the foundation of all we've known about the later years. It's unlikely our finances will stretch long enough to provide for the comforts we'd like at age 92; it's even less likely we'll travel this portion of life's journey without some health challenges. It's implausible that we'll fully disengage from some form of work like our parents and past generations did; and, perhaps most importantly, it's questionable that we have a serious plan for this third stage of life. How could we, anyway! This is pioneering territory for all of us.

Consider our emerging reality – by 2030 one out of every five Americans will be over the age of 65. Imagine how this impacts the workforce! Our corporations will not be able to survive unless there is a rapid movement to capture the older worker, to accommodate to the needs of the older worker, and to build programs that are attractive to us. CVS Pharmacy is one of a growing number of companies creating innovative approaches to harness the power of the growing over-65 population – they have a 'snowbird' program that allows the older worker to take the winter months off or to find work in 'snowbird country' if they are headed in that direction.

Improbable and costly as it seems, companies will soon need to re-examine attitudes toward retaining older workers in significant leadership positions with all of their high salaries and benefits. It's today's practice to cut the cord and look down the ranks for younger and more affordable leadership talent, but demographics are not on the side of the corporation on this strategy. At some point between today and 2030, the pipeline will be nearly empty.

I remember getting a call not so long ago from a gentleman who had been through one of our seminars. He had planned his retirement from a professional practice, and he and his wife put together plans for some much longed-for traveling and freedom from the day-to-day constraints of running a long time practice. He had a great retirement party, he was appreciated by an entire community that he had dedicated himself to for over forty years, and it was with deep satisfaction that he walked out of his office for the last time, closed the door and headed off with his wife to adventure for awhile.

The travels eventually came to an end, he and his wife returned home, life for everyone but him seemed to return to its usual pace and rhythm – so what was the problem? He put it like this, *It's not a vacation when you return to a life without work;*

I dare you, man of affairs, to have a magnificent obsession.

— William Danforth

what's more, once I re-landed into our routines, I looked around and noticed for the first time in my life that all of my friends were still at the medical practice working, and I had cultivated virtually no friends outside of my work life. Even worse, I had cultivated no activities beyond those related to running a dental practice. So now what – how do I start all over again at 65?

We neither get better or worse as we get older, but more like ourselves.

— Robert Anthony

Our dentist, John, didn't know where to begin, and the best information he had was that he once had enormous passion for his work, his profession, his contributions to others; he also had great pride and a sense of purpose from raising his family and all the activities that went along with that from infancy to graduate school and beyond.

Knowing something about how it is to feel fully alive, on fire, engaged and passionate about our days is important information - this is a starting point for any of us. Next, we need to believe that passion is not only possible but essential in this third stage of life or we will grow old as bored boomers who are unable to create a new sense of purpose that is fulfilling to us and a give-back to others.

The word 'retirement' is derived from the French *retirer,* which literally means 'to withdraw' or 'to go into seclusion'. While we haven't landed on the term that best captures this new time of our 60's, 70's and beyond in the twenty-first century, most of us are clear that neither the old concept or the term 'retirement' reflects the complexities and opportunities we confront today.

We do know we are living longer, healthier, more vital lives than past generations and we aren't content to engage in a decade or two of leisure activities. Some are ready to pursue unlived dreams of much earlier years, others have little choice but to continue to work and rebuild the 'nest egg', and yet others want to divest of life's clutter and find ways to make a difference in the world.

This stage requires a stiff dose of courage in order to step out of the 'comfort zone' of life. By the time we reach this phase of life we are steeped in habits and routines and shaking loose is hard to do! Yet, the much used phrase –"if not now, when?" – grabs our attention like never before and the choice is ours.

Blueprint for Recasting in the Third Launch

- Craft your narrative. A little like writing your memoir, take some time to 'tell' yourself your story on paper. Write from several perspectives – perhaps through the eye of another (your partner, a good friend, or a mentor). Review your writing and notice the themes, the surprises, the spaces that get your attention.

- Test an outrageous dream – if not now, when? Think back to your 'youngest you' when you were in those intoxicating adolescent years –– what were your dreams and is now the time to try on one or two?

- Stay committed to your health. The pace of health challenges quickens at this stage in life and as the saying goes "without your health, you've got nothing". Trite as it sounds, it's a fact – so daily routines that keep us as fit and healthy as possible are a must. If you don't have a routine and you've never had the 'exercise' habit – start now, begin with small steps and notice the difference you'll feel within just a few weeks.

- Make money work for you. Be smart, be realistic. Understand your financial realities and adjust accordingly.

- Test out new kinds of work. Maybe you've long had a dream that is vastly different than all you've done and been thus far in life. This is the time to test the water!

- Think openly about your death. Longevity is partially informed by family history, so start there. Make a guesstimate about the age at which you'll die. Now count the number of years you've got between then and now. How do you want to view your life at the time of your death? What do you need to attend to now?

- What's your legacy? Most of us won't leave a building or a big business, but legacy takes many forms from the most personal to the public. What legacy do you dream of leaving for your children? Is the life you're living creating that legacy? What would you want your children to remember you by when you're gone? What will the world at large remember?

To be young is to be fresh, lively, eager, quick to learn; to be mature is to be done, complete, sedate, tired. What if we consider a different perspective? To be young is to be unripe, unfinished, raw, awkward, unskilled, inept; to be mature is to be ready, whole, adept, wise. How valid are our glorification of youth and our shame about having lived many years?

— Lillian E. Troll

The adult journey lasts longer and is more vibrant than ever before in history. We are free from many of the social constraints of past generations and the variations on the themes and contours of our many decades is intoxicating and liberating; and at times daunting as well. Today, change is a predictable part of our lives, and the speed and intensity of change calls each of us to be more deliberate and intentional about how we want our lives to unfold at each step along the journey. Life is filled with unexpected surprises – and yet, it's our inner sense of direction and purpose that helps us stay on course.

Chapter Eight

Map 5

The Adult Learning Agenda
Becoming the Best that You Can Be

In a world that is constantly changing, there is no one subject or set of subjects that will serve you for the foreseeable future, let alone for the rest of your life. The most important skill to acquire now is learning how to learn. — John Naisbitt

The Adult Learning Agenda
Becoming the Best that You Can Be

The Learning Map completes your preparation for creating a new chapter.

In Map 1 you gained mastery over your experience of change so that you can find increased comfort and effectiveness with the turbulence of today.

Map 2 led you to choose your emerging priorities for the next chapter of your life. You identified your core values and your compelling sense of purpose.

Map 3 helped you reappraise your social activities and roles–the strategic assignments in which you can best find fulfillment at this time in your life. Relating your key roles to your current core values is essential to a healthy LifeLaunch.

Map 4 added an understanding of the complexities of the adult journey and the handful of crisis points that invite you into new decisions and new ways of being in life at each step in the unfolding process.

Map 5 is a cornucopia of adult learning ingredients, from which you pick and choose those important items that will illuminate your path and improve your skills and sense of competence for the next chapter. Your best future is discovered and invented through the all-important learning lens.

> *The only person who is educated is the one who has learned how to learn…and change.*
>
> — Carl Rogers

The Adult Learning Agenda   Map Five

___ **1.** What do I need to unlearn?

___ **2.** What new information do I need?

___ **3.** How do I increase my personal confidence?

___ **4.** What new technical skills do I need?

___ **5.** How can I stay anchored in my values?

___ **6.** Where are my best learning environments?

___ **7.** Who are my real teachers and mentors?

Tell me, I'll forget.
Show me, I may
remember.
But involve me and
I'll understand.

— Chinese Proverb

Fully engaged adults are always learning. Absorbing new knowledge or skills is an attitude, a habit, and a way of life. To learn is to turn problems into investigations, and crises into opportunities. When you are learning you discover new ways to approach unknown territory, and you subdue any fear of uncertainties in your life.

Learning is self-initiated change, wherein you develop fresh capabilities and replace out-dated thinking with new ideas. Learning helps you gain increased comfort with newness everywhere in your life. When you are engaged in the art of learning, the changing world around you seems less threatening. In an age of extraordinary turbulence, learning is the most important human modality for empowering adult life.

Few of us use learning to our full advantage. It is all too easy to lock ourselves into what we've already learned as the world spins on into new paradigms. Many of us replace our youthful habits for learning with midlife habits of unwinding on evenings and weekends, leaving new learning to others. You have a choice: rest on your oars and let your boat drift along, or keep learning new nautical skills so you can proceed to preferred destinations.

Adult learning is about discovering, not memorizing. It's about awakening, not passing tests. It's about visceral discovery, not mental schooling. Adult learning is frequently related to experiential development, not to formal instruction or teaching. It is self-directed inquiry, reflection, and application.

Real learning unleashes joy and excitement, confidence and determination, in addition to acquiring new skills and competencies. Learning links you to future possibilities and paths for moving ahead.

Learning also addresses the fear of aging. Adults at any age who fail to keep up with the acceleration of learning take on stereotypical "old" behaviors – passivity, fear, and lowered self-esteem. Continuous learning keeps you vital, awake, and expectant.

Adult Learning Questions in Six Key Areas

Before you launched your first fully adult chapter in life, you went to school for years to prepare for the great adventure ahead – your adult years. You earned degrees, got work experience, learned how to manage yourself in many settings, became an expert in something, and settled down for the long haul.

Your training for that first chapter took somewhere close to twenty years, and when you launched your dream you may have lacked experience, but you didn't lack careful preparation and powerful determination.

The chief object of education is not to learn things but to unlearn things.

— G.K. Chesterton

During the rest of your life you will have lots of experience, but probably little new and significant learning preparation, unless you make it happen. Society wound you up for the first launching, but you have to wind yourself up for every subsequent chapter. There are *helpful questions to ask yourself* in six key areas to define the new learning you need before designing your plan for the next chapter of your life.

Your Turn!

In your journal or notebook, identify your learning objectives for the next chapter of your life using the format below to guide you in answering the questions in these six areas:

1. UNLEARNING. What do I have to unlearn if I'm going to master the future I truly want? What patterns of thinking that served me well earlier in my life are now in the way of what I really want to do and become?

How do you discover what you need to unlearn? Take some time to consider the following set of questions. Take some notes, jot down some reactions over the course of a week or two:

- **Ask yourself,** "What am I resisting the most? What can I do to become proactive in that part of my life? What small steps could I begin to take?"

- **Ask your friends** what they think you need to unlearn – this may seem a little uncomfortable, but good friends 'see' things you can't see about yourself. Listen and take advantage of their wisdom.

- **Ask your boss and co-workers** what you need to unlearn – this will help you build even stronger career pathways now and in the future.

- **Commit time** at least once a year to attend a conference or seminar where the cutting edge of what interests you is the theme. As you sit and listen to new perspectives and ideas, ask yourself the question, "What do I need to unlearn, in order to break out of my set patterns, so I can continue to develop instead of merely holding on?"

Learning is a willingness to let one's ability and attitude change in response to new ideas, information and experiences.

— Peter Vaill

2. NEW INFORMATION AND KNOWLEDGE. What *new information and knowledge* do I need in order to be at my best *at this time in my life?* What information and knowledge can I legitimately *avoid* in order to prevent information overload?

In our kind of world you have to keep up in the areas of your special concerns, and filter out the clamor of the world that has little to do with the path you are on. The secret to acquiring new information and knowledge is to focus on those areas in which you want continuous information and cutting-edge expertise.

The flip-side is saying no to the endless intrusions upon your learning time, particularly the profusion of information accessible online today. If it doesn't inform the path you're on, or add meaning to your life, just say no! Try out some of these tried and true methods for continuing to build your pool of knowledge:

- **Read, read, read.** Seek out new sources for your reading including books, articles, online news, blogs and more. Make your reading schedule the steady core of your learning agenda and join reading groups so you can discuss new ideas with others.

- **Social networks.** They are everywhere and it can get overwhelming to sort through the most valuable resources. Be discriminating, find one or two that appeals to you and connects you to a vital community of people. Don't be afraid to experiment – the list of options today is endless and the key is finding the ones that work for you and link you to new thinking and great ideas.

- **Intensive seminars and workshops.** Instead of the standard 'soup of the day' variety, invest in three to five day group learning formats that engage you profoundly in your own learning and development.

- **Episodic learning.** Travel alone, climb a mountain, take an adventure, conduct a vision quest, or join one of the 'travel and volunteer' trips sponsored by several organizations worldwide. Spend some time working and living in other parts of the world. Discover how people very different from you live and work. Jolt your routines to discover new ones that connect you better to the future.

- **Advanced certifications and degree programs.** Advanced learning programs for midlife and older adults are growing at a rapid pace. Educational institutions are devising ways for adults to maintain current commitments and routines while pursuing a certification or degree. These programs typically offer intensive learning opportunities in tandem with professional and personal renewal, new collegial friendships, and new perspectives.

> *Self-education is, I firmly believe, the only kind of education there is.*
>
> — Isaac Asimov

3. PERSONAL COMPETENCE. What *life skills* do I want and need to develop, to be alive and purposive in all that I do?

Life skills refer to our general human abilities to sustain relationships, be an effective parent, manage conflict, travel, and feel at home in the world. Life skills are abilities like listening, speaking, writing, negotiating, and more. Today's world has many technocrats and executives who have outstanding behaviors in their specialized fields, but who haven't learned the basic human skills for managing the many parts of their own lives. It's never too late to learn new life skills that enhance and broaden your sense of personal competence. Consider some the suggestions below for stretching your sense of personal competence:

*No man can reveal
to you but that
which already lies
half asleep in the
dawning of your
knowledge.*

— Khalil Gibran

- **Hire a coach.** Target an area or two you'd like to strengthen, build some goals and work with a coach to systematically grow your capacity. Coaches are equipped to help you reach bold new goals, make small adjustments or tackle some specific new ways of being in the world. At The Hudson Institute we have nearly a thousand coaches around the globe who have trained with us and who provide outstanding coaching services to adults in transition.

- **Invest in psychotherapy.** We are all served by understanding the inner terrain, the scripts and the inevitable dreams and limitations we live inside. Psychotherapy offers an opportunity to deepen your understanding of self, and in the process you expand your options in living.

- **Take some assessments.** Try out an assessment or two to increase your awareness of what areas you might target for your own development. Whether it's a temperament inventory such as the well-known Myers Briggs, an emotional intelligence EQ assessment, a conflict profile, or any other assessment that reveals helpful information for you to use in your continual development.

4. VALUES AND LEADERSHIP ROLES. What do I need to learn to keep my life *aligned to my values and leadership roles?*

Sooner or later, you become a leader – of yourself and perhaps much more. You engage your values through acts of inspiration, persuasion, and example. Leadership does not have to be full-time or all consuming; it needs to be fulfilling and meaningful. True leadership grows out of your own integrity and concerns, not polls or desired rewards. Most midlife and elder adults want to become a positive influence within the culture around them – through children and grandchildren, organizations they believe in, and the political process itself.

Leadership begins when you lead your own human agenda in a purposive way. Leadership is anchored in your deep, dependable qualities, not in memorized affirmations or roles. Start with personal leadership, and you will soon find all kinds of ways to exert influence beyond yourself.

- **Find an apprenticeship** – this is particularly helpful in the early chapters as it provides a sense of what you can expect in particular career domains.

- **Take an internship** – this is another great way to test waters you haven't traveled in before.

- **Take on a leadership role in your community** – this combines contribution with your own leadership development, and if you plan it carefully, you can pursue leadership skills in arenas that add to your current work.

- **Volunteer for a cause that you care about** – this is perhaps one of the simplest ways to take action in this arena. You can volunteer one time or on an ongoing basis and it's always easy to find causes that need help!

- **Join a leadership group** – there are many options from which to choose including community leadership groups, national leadership organizations, leadership intensives and more.

Knowledge is power.

— Francis Bacon

5. LEARNING ENVIRONMENTS. Where are the learning environments and resources that I need at this time in my life?

Since our global village is your campus today, scope out your best learning centers and formats – seminars, online modules, mentors, conferences, books, study groups, certification programs, advanced degrees, travel/study programs – and get yourself connected.

Don't think of learning as something you have to purchase from some teacher or educational service. Learning is what you need to acquire because you are ready, and you are in charge of how you do the acquiring!

There is a Chinese saying that when the pupil is ready, the teacher will appear. The same is true for learning environments. When you're ready to learn, the learning opportunity will appear.

6. TEACHERS AND MENTORS. Who are *my teachers and mentors*, at this time in my life?

Adults do not want to sit at the feet of mere knowledge experts, they want to learn from masters – persons who have applied knowledge to themselves and their professions, people who have unconscious competence integrated into their behavior.

That is why so many conventional college professors do not appeal to midlife adults as appropriate teachers. They are often experts in a cognitive field of study, not masters of how that field connects to life around them. Adult students want to apply knowledge and gain mastery beyond that knowledge.

The new adult teacher is a mentor, 'mensch', or master – someone who lives and breathes "viscerally" what the learner wants to learn. You will grow in new ways in the presence of a mentor, and at all stages in the adult journey we benefit from their presence. It's a two way street, the mentor doesn't simply *appear* one day. You need to scan your world, get intentional and seek out mentors who will matter and make a difference in your journey.

Learning is remaining fully alive at all stages in life's journey. Learning only begins in our formal educational systems, and the ongoing 'real-time' learning we initiate ourselves is an essential ingredient in leading a fully-awake life. In fact, ongoing learning that we orchestrate ourselves is probably one of the single most important activities that allows us to live effectively in these changing times.

To be a human being is to be a continual learner all of one's life.

— Peter Vaill

Section Three

Launching a New Chapter

Chapter Nine

Map 6

The Vision, Purpose and Plan
Get a Plan
Walk Your Talk

When you are inspired by some great purpose, some extraordinary project, all your thoughts break their bounds: Your mind transcends limitations, your consciousness expands in every direction and you find yourself in a new, great and wonderful world. Dormant forces, faculties and talents become alive, and you discover yourself to be a greater person by far than you ever dreamed yourself to be. — Patanjali

The Vision, Purpose and Plan
Get a Plan – Walk Your Talk

THE LIFELAUNCH FORMULA

STEP 1

FEEL YOUR SENSE OF PURPOSE
The Awe and Mystery of the Not-Yet
Tap Your Inner Energy
"I am alive and expectant."
Purpose is your WHY.

STEP 2

IMAGINE THE FUTURE YOU PREFER
Vision, Dream, Picture, Wonder
Identify Your Core Values, Your Deep Passions
"I am drawn irresistibly to this direction."
Vision is your WHAT.

STEP 3

CREATE WORDS AND REALITY PATHS TO GUIDE YOU
Translate your dreams and goals into Your Story
Identify The Most Important Roles in Your Life Now
Make a Plan to Get from Here to There
Create Action Steps and Time Lines
"I/We will do and become it."
Plans are your HOW.

IF you can imagine it, you can achieve it.
IF you can dream it, you can become it.

— William A. Ward

This chapter guides you through the steps to follow as you put together the details of your next chapter, your LifeLaunch. First, give some thought to how you might sabotage your plan or be sabotaged by unanticipated outside forces.

Take a Look at What Might Go Wrong

It's one thing to get a good fix on how you want your next chapter in life to be and quite another to make it happen. As you nudge your way closer to planning and launching, it's vitally important to take a good look at the dark sides of yourself and the world around you, noticing what could go wrong. A careful attention to the obstacles allows you to stand ready for the natural adversities that appear when you decide to make a change.

Homeostasis happens. Even when you decide you want a change you will find yourself challenged to take the needed risks, and your environment and all the important players in your current chapter like things just as they are. So the forces of homeostasis (the draw toward stability and what we know) are at work drawing you toward your past – what you've known, what you've been, and all the habits you've developed over time.

The unknown can be unnerving territory. You know how to 'do' your current chapter and oddly enough, even when it's no longer satisfying, it often seems easier than venturing into unknown territory. It's far easier to take this leap if you are clear about what you are reaching for and aspiring to in the new chapter ahead. Your goals and aspirations become your all-important anchor in the swirl of change.

The voice of the inner board of directors. You may not always notice it, but you've got your own internal board of directors – we all do! If you listen carefully to the voices on your board, you'll notice how many are supportive of this change you are planning, and how many are scaring you and warning you about the dangers of the unknown. It's helpful to uncover these voices – you might decide it's time to re-arrange your board of directors!

While we can't eliminate all of the obstacles and boulders on our path, we can be far more alert to them and learn how to live with them more creatively. Often this gives you the upper hand! Here are some planning steps that will help you manage the inescapable obstacles and boulders you'll encounter:

First of all, put the obstacles and boulders on your path into two groups: external threats and internal obstacles.

Second, examine the external threats and internal obstacles that might subvert your plans for the new chapter ahead to see how you might get around them.

Third, build specific strategies into your plan for managing your external threats and internal obstacles.

External Threats

An external threat is something that comes at you from the world around you. These are the natural reality issues we simply can't avoid. We've all got them and the bigger these threats, the harder it is to break through, manage them and make change happen in your life. Yet it's always true that understanding the threats makes it easier to creatively deal with them. So for starters, take a look at the list of External Threats and check the ones that apply and will likely make changes more challenging.

Dreams have as much influence as actions.

— Stephanie Mallarme

Your Ratings:

Column 1
Serious Threat

Column 2
Manageable Threat

Column 3
Potential Threat

External Threats	*Your Ratings*		
	1	2	3
Financial Responsibilities	☐	☐	☐
Family Constraints	☐	☐	☐
College Expenses	☐	☐	☐
College Loans	☐	☐	☐
Spouse's Lack of Support	☐	☐	☐
Children's School Situation	☐	☐	☐
Aging Parents	☐	☐	☐
Health Issues	☐	☐	☐
Caregiving Responsibilities	☐	☐	☐
Lack of Adequate Savings	☐	☐	☐
Potential Loss of Full Pension	☐	☐	☐
Health Insurance Problems	☐	☐	☐
Looming Divorce	☐	☐	☐
Current Job Market	☐	☐	☐
Lack of Work Experience	☐	☐	☐
Lack of Contacts	☐	☐	☐
Recession Concerns	☐	☐	☐
My Age	☐	☐	☐
Being Fired	☐	☐	☐
Being Downsized	☐	☐	☐
Drinking Problems	☐	☐	☐
Other	☐	☐	☐
Other	☐	☐	☐
Other	☐	☐	☐

Internal Obstacles

An internal obstacle is something you do to make it difficult to reach your goals and to feel good. It's the 'board of directors' in all of us. We've all got internal habits and stories that get activated when we want to make big changes. Some possible internal obstacles you might want to consider are found on the list below. Rate each one on a scale of 1 to 3 with 1 being significant obstacle, 2 being somewhat of an obstacle, and 3 being an occasional obstacle.

Internal Obstacles	Your Ratings		
	1	2	3
Financial Responsibilities	☐	☐	☐
Old Habits	☐	☐	☐
Past Failure(s)	☐	☐	☐
Current Success	☐	☐	☐
Sense of Hopelessness	☐	☐	☐
Denial	☐	☐	☐
Depression	☐	☐	☐
Anger	☐	☐	☐
Blaming	☐	☐	☐
Sense of Helplessness	☐	☐	☐
Low Self Esteem	☐	☐	☐
Stress	☐	☐	☐
Fear	☐	☐	☐
Lack of Time Management	☐	☐	☐
Procrastination	☐	☐	☐
Lack of Focus	☐	☐	☐
Perfectionism	☐	☐	☐
Victim Story	☐	☐	☐

If you don't design your own life plan, chances are you'll fall into someone else's. And guess what they have planned for you – not much!

— Jim Rohr

Your Ratings:

Column 1
Significant Obstacle

Column 2
Somewhat
of an Obstacle

Column 3
Occasional Obstacle

How can you learn to remove these obstacles on your path, particularly those you rated 1 or 2? Interestingly enough, once you are consciously aware of the obstacles that get in your way, you gain some control over them. Once you've 'named' the obstacles, you won't be surprised when they show up, you can get creative about managing them, and you can be a stronger support to yourself in the midst of change.

Now that you've identified the real external threats and internal obstacles that you are likely to face in the next chapter of your life, ask yourself the following questions, and come up with initial answers you can count on *before* you write your plan. Write out your responses in your journal or notebook:

What are Your External Threats?

1. What are your major worries about the world you are living in right now? How do your specific circumstances and realities affect you and reduce your effectiveness? What is the story you tell yourself that may create an obstacle for you? How might you change the way you let your reality issues reduce your ability to take a step forward?

2. To what extent are your "external threats" actually stories you've brought with you from the past?

3. Which ones are, in fact, threatening your future and need to be addressed in some way so you can believe in your future possibilities?

What are Your Internal Obstacles?

1. How have you messed up your own plans or got in your own way in years past? How does your personal pattern, script or subversion work? If you really don't know, ask someone who knows you well and how they see you.

2. Knowing you can't totally eliminate all of your negative and unsupportive thoughts, beliefs, stories and habits, how might you seek to minimize their negative impact on your next chapter?

3. Who are the persons you can count on to help you think through internal obstacles and/or external threats that get in the way of your plan? Identify your critical support system now. We all need people in our lives to encourage and sustain us in times of change.

Summarize Your Findings from the Maps

Before engaging in the work of the final map (Map 6) – writing a plan for the next chapter of your life, make a summary in your journal or notebook of what you've gleaned thus far from the five maps we've covered. Use the outline below as a guideline. If you already have these findings clearly in mind, move right ahead with this chapter.

MAP 1
Composing Life Chapters and Transitions
The Cycle of Renewal

1. Are you currently in a life chapter or in a transition time in your life? (see pages 52-54)?

2. Which of the phases are you in (see pages 55-68)?

☐ **Phase One – Going For It**, challenged by a new beginning, clear goals, and available resources.

☐ **Phase Two – Stuck in the Doldrums**, sensing decline, resisting change, feeling disenchanted.

☐ **Mini-transition** – Improving the current chapter you are in by making minor adjustments.

☐ **Phase Three – Cocooning**, taking time out to heal, renew yourself and tap your core values.

☐ **Phase Four – Getting Ready**, exploring the world again through learning, experimenting, networking, training and getting ready for Phase One again.

MAP 2
Leading a Deliberate Life
Living with Passion and Purpose

3. List in order of importance, from one (the highest) to six (the lowest) your core values for the next chapter of your life (see pages 80-81):

_____ Personal Power
_____ Achievement
_____ Intimacy
_____ Play and Creativity
_____ Search for Meaning
_____ Compassion and Contribution

4. Indicate some of the **results or passionate destinations** you want during the next chapter of your life, from the top three core values just indicated.

5. On page 88 you translated your core values into a "purpose statement" for the next chapter of your life. Review what you wrote in your journal or notebook and either endorse it and use it – if what you wrote remains valid and compelling, or write a more alive and relevant version that expresses your sense of purpose at this time.

MAP 3
Life's Assignments
Balancing the Parts of Your Life

6. Indicate those activities, roles, and commitments that are most important for the next chapter of your life in each category (see pages 94-101).

☐ **Personal** (List commitments and activities in this category that are important for your next chapter.)

☐ **Couple/Partner** (List commitments and activities in this category that are important for your next chapter.)

☐ **Family** (List commitments, roles and activities in this category that are important for your next chapter.)

☐ **Friends** (List commitments and activities in this category that are important for your next chapter.)

☐ **Work** (List commitments, roles, and activities in this category that are important for your next chapter.)

☐ **Community** (List commitments, roles and activities in this category that are important for your next chapter.)

7. How do you want to deliberately change any of these important roles and the activities and commitments that accompany them in your next chapter?

MAP 4
The Grand Journey
Across the Life Cycle

8. What are your central developmental challenges and potential crisis points at this time in your life – the current invitations for deepening your life? How might you embrace any crisis point in your chapter ahead? What are your emergent forces, concerns, values, and spiritual direction for the next chapter of your life?

MAP 5
The Adult Learning Agenda
Becoming the Best You Can Be

9. What are your responses to the Six Key Adult Learning Questions (see pages 135-140)?

☐ What do I need to unlearn?

☐ What new information do I need?

☐ What areas do I need to work to increase my personal competence?

☐ What are my core values and how do I translate these into my leadership roles?

☐ What are my best learning environments?

☐ Who are my real teachers and mentors?

10. What are my strategic learning plans for the next chapter of my life?

11. Summarize your learning agenda.

MAP 6
Vision, Purpose and Plan
Putting It All Together

Examine the summary you've just made, and your entire journal or notebook, to see if there are goals or actions steps that should go into your plan.

Now: put each goal or action step on a 'post-it' sticky and attach it to a wall or large sheet of paper where you can do your final planning. This way you can see all the planning possibilities you've already identified as you move into full-time planning and putting it all together – the work of Map 6.

How Will the Next Chapter of Your Life Unfold?

1. If you were granted one wish for the next chapter of your life, what would it be?

2. If you could live out the next chapter of your life in any place in the world, where would you go?

3. If you could choose one or two mentors to guide the next chapter of your life, who would they be?

4. If you could move now to some future point in your life, what are you doing and who is with you?

5. If you have children, how would you like to be in relation to them five years from now?

6. If you were recognized as an enormous success at the end of the next chapter of your life, what would you be known for?

7. If you could have friends attribute one quality to you at the end of the next chapter of your life, what would you want it to be?

8. If you could provide a title for the next chapter of your life, what would it be?

The remainder of this chapter is devoted to the heart of Map 6, our proven process for creating a detailed plan for yourself that will lead to a successful launch of the next chapter in your life. Make sure to take your time and follow it systematically using these three important steps:

- Identify your purpose
- Write your vision of the future you prefer
- Write your detailed plan for the next chapter

Step 1
What Is Your Purpose at this Time in Your Life?

Purpose, Vision, and Plans are like three doors leading to a new chapter in your life. The first of these is "purpose," your raison d'être, your answer to "Why am I here?"

No one has much of a life without hope and belief in the future.

Purpose is a profound commitment to a compelling expectation for this time in your life.

No one has the same sense of purpose throughout an entire life. You conceive of new facets of your purpose at different ages and phases of your life.

- Purpose is not the same as goals. It is a greater force than goals, and less precise.

- Purpose is an expression of your ultimate concerns.

- Purpose is the sum of your yearnings for what you may become, or devote your life to becoming.

- Purpose comes from your basic belief system, whatever it is.

- Purpose inspires the activities of your life.

- Purpose provides meaning for your life.

- Purpose generates commitment beyond your daily needs to the most lofty reaches of your mind and soul.

You feel your sense of purpose deep within you, in what Carl Jung called your inner "self," that part of you that transcends your ego needs and connects you to lasting values and meaning. Purpose, which is anchored in "being," provides meaning to "doing," "loving," and "playing." Some people find purpose through their faith, but people who live without a religious belief system need purpose just as much as religious believers. Our lives don't function well or long without a deeper purpose.

After reviewing what you said about your purpose in life, in Map 2 on page 81, update your statement of purpose for the next chapter of your life. Write it out in your journal or notebook. Keep it simple, short, and compelling. Rewrite it until it feels like a magnet pulling you ahead. Talk it over with your closest friends, because while purpose is highly personal, it is also social and spiritual.

Step 2
What Is Your Vision or Dream for the Next Chapter of Your Life?

Your purpose distills into a vision or dream, which is more precise and clear than your purpose, but less exact and clear than your plan. You almost always begin a new chapter of life with a dream. "We hold these truths to be self-evident," said a founding father of our country, as he laid out the American dream that has been a major social force guiding our country for over 200 years. "I have a dream," yearned Martin Luther King in Washington, D.C., as he painted a picture of equality and fairness in America, and made it his full time agenda.

The dream comes first. Reality chases after the dream, to make it happen.

- A vision or dream declares what is important, purposive, and valuable for your life ahead.

- It is a poetic picture, not a literal statement.

- A vision or dream is visceral yearning, not a wish list. You don't dream for a new car, an exotic vacation, or even a new career. Rather, you envision in your mind's eye an overall picture for your future life – working, living, contributing, and having fun.

- A vision is a spiritual promise of a new quality of life, a deeper sense of being, a value-added life. It's a promise that is convincing. To think it, is to begin to go for it. It feels right, and it's going to happen, because it's already happening. It feels that simple and compelling.

- A real vision feels like it is pulling you toward it from without and pushing you towards it from within. Like a sail it guides you toward the shores you need to reach; like a rudder it guides you–a day at a time–with an innate sense of direction.

- A dream is a haunting refrain. You know you have a vision when it won't let you go, and others are attracted to it in you.

- A dream inspires and motivates; it doesn't order you around. As far as we know, human beings are the only creatures on earth capable of envisioning a future and then setting about to make it happen.

- A dream is energy as much as it is anything else, a grasp on everything you want to happen – or not happen.

Instructions for Visioning

Go to some favorite place, preferably in a natural setting where you are alone and not pressured by other responsibilities and time constraints. Relax and allow your mind to see how you want your next chapter to emerge in all its important dimensions – your personal life, your important activities, the people you are connected to, and anything else of great importance in your life at this time.

Give yourself permission to dream without censoring yourself around money, time, or other pressing issues. Simply imagine your preferred future, with you at your best. Ask yourself questions like these:

- Where will I be geographically?

- Who will be with me?

- What will I be about?

- What will be important for me, providing meaning and happiness and security?

- How will I be at work? Home? Play? Travel? Creative activities?

Let your vision touch everything. Make it a central dream that informs all of your life. Review it over and over until the same vision or dream keeps repeating itself, to your continued delight. Then get your notebook or journal and write down every detail and aspect of your dream.

Write out your vision or dream for the next chapter of your life as a story or drama unfolding. Let it have elegance and even a bit of grandiosity, so that you can relish its flavor and richness. Let it have the power to inspire, enrapture, and pull you into it during the next few years.

Step 3
What Is Your Plan
for the Next Chapter of Your Life?

If purpose is the source of your deepest affirmations, and visioning is how you picture your optimal possibilities for the near future, planning is how you implement the vision in the real world, *now.*

- Purpose is spiritual, value-based, and motivating, although often not immediately applicable. It is your "why".

- Visioning is dreamy, pictorial, imaginative, soft-headed, energy releasing, and not literal. It is more definite than purpose but not yet directly applicable to daily living. It is your "what."

- Planning is realistic, logical, hard-headed, definite, factual, literal, and time-driven. It is your "how." When you plan, you take your purpose and dream and break it down into goals, objectives, action steps, and time lines. Planning is a step-by-step process for making the dream happen, with a little worldly savvy thrown in.

To create a future, the dream must become a plan, as the dreamer becomes a planner. Planning is more than a bunch of skills; it is an inner force, a felt competence, a strength within us. The planner pushes forward with logical steps, like choosing reliable stepping stones to cross a stream. Through strategic thinking, the planner embroiders the dreamer's vision in the complexity of the world, weaving together technical and human resources required to bring the new chapter into reality. The possible dream becomes a probable plan.

A plan is a living document, not a stone etching. Frequent evaluation is required, along with adaptation to new resources and opportunities as they are discovered. Yet the basic plan will remain, as a vehicle for making the dream happen. Plans need to be definite, anchored carefully in a sequence of events and a committed life with time management.

First, conduct an inventory (below) of what activities you want to include in the next chapter of your life. Then plunge into the planning process and define your plan.

Planning Item: An Activities Inventory

Integrate the information you have obtained from this book by forming three sets of potential action steps for your future: what to hold on to, what to let go of, and what to take on. Make lists in your notebook or journal, with as many items as you want under each heading:

HOLD ON
Activities you want to do more of

LET GO
Activities you want to do less of, or stop doing altogether

TAKE ON
New activities you want to begin

Planning Item: Prepare Your Planning Cards

Get a pack of 3"x5" index cards or post-its and create a Planning Card on as many cards as you want for your plan. Each card will represent one goal or objective. Don't overwhelm yourself with too many cards. Seek to identify your most important strategic steps ahead, and let them lead you – throughout the plan – to more cards. Use a heavy rubber band around them so you can carry them in your purse or briefcase and review them each week.

We call these cards "stepping stones" because each one represents a destination on your preferred path. Don't rush to fill out the cards. Just prepare them for making a plan, filling out your preferred "stepping stones" for your journey ahead. Here is the grid to use on one side of each card:

Planning Card

Completion Date

Stepping Stone *(goal or objective)*

Action Steps   Dates

1.

2.

3.

Now, Construct Your Plan,
and Build Your New Chapter
in the Following Sequence

• **Identify the stepping stones** that will lead you as surely as you know how from where you are toward your vision. Place one stepping stone goal or objective on each card, exhausting your sense of the results you want to obtain from your plan before you spend any time on action steps and time management issues.

• **Identify a completion date for each stepping stone.** In the upper right hand corner of each card that you intend to use, indicate the deadline date when you want and expect this goal to be realized.

- **Create three simple, challenging action steps** for each card. Under each goal list three action steps and dates which you will take to realize each goal. Keep each step small and easy so you don't overwhelm yourself. Concentrate only on three action steps. When you complete a step, create a new one – 4, or 5, or 6 on the back side – so you always have three action steps and their dates in front of you until you reach your goal by the completion date in the upper right hand corner. Use the back of the card or new cards as needed.

- **Organize your cards.** Spread them out on a table (or put them on a wall if available), so you can see them as a whole. Then invent some organizing principle that works for you: chronologically, or by topics, or by your values, or by your systems and roles. After you've completed your planning cards to your initial satisfaction, organize them into various patterns (passions, roles, chronology, or other categories that make sense to you) until you are convinced that you have the stepping stones you need and want to empower your next chapter.

- **Rehearse your plan.** Be sure that your ultimate plan is your story or script, not merely a bunch of busy activities. Rehearse your cards over and over until you feel at home in your story for the next year or two of your life. Let your plan fulfill your mission, and your mission lead to your dream or vision. Remember that continual rehearsing of your plan turns you into an anticipatory person, ready to make your future happen.

- **Enter each "action step" into your planning system.** When your plan is congruent with your purpose, your vision, and your mission, enter each action step into whatever sort of calendaring system you use, with evaluation points every three months. Put copies of your purpose, vision, and mission statements in your calendaring system, along with photos, doodling and small artwork that represent your next chapter in life. Turn your calendaring system into your life planning system as well!

- **Network to facilitate your future.** Build a network of support that will assist you as you step into your new chapter and speed the process as well. Cast a wide net, imaging a circle with layers starting at the core and extending to the perimeters. Use your network in different ways depending upon what layer they reside in. You may have several acquaintances in the outer rings that could provide contacts about some of the less personal dimensions of your new chapter, while those at the center are reserved for what requires more commitment to you and longer conversations over time.

Your walk through these maps or lenses is a journey through each of the elements of a whole person – ever changing, always in motion. First in Map 1 you looked at the ongoing cycle of change and renewal at play at all times in your life – this provides context for your actions and decisions. Next you grounded yourself in Map 2 – your deepest sense of purpose, asking at each step in your journey what matters most now, and using this as fuel for your evolving plans. Map 3 allowed you to examine which roles and systems you are invested in at any given time, while Map 4 reminded you of the ever changing landscape of the adult journey. Map 5 prompted you to view learning as a 'way of being' in the world today, and Map 6 linked your hopes, dreams, realities and stage in life with a purposeful action plan for the chapter ahead.

Section Four

Resources for a LifeLaunch

A READING LIST
FOR EMBRACING THE FUTURE

MIND-CHANGING BOOKS

Arrien, Angeles. *The Second Half of Life.* Boulder: Sounds True, Inc., 2005. Arrien introduces Eight Gates of Initiation with steps through each gate to deepen your most valuable relationships, reclaim your untended creative talents, and shift your focus from ambition to meaning.

Beck, Martha. The Joy Diet – 10 Daily Practices for a Happier Life. New York: Crown Publishers, 2003. Beck offers a menu of ten behaviors to enhance every day's journey through the unpredictable terrain of existence.

D'Amico, Barbara. *No More Default Judgments: Recapturing the Dream.* Law Practice Magazine, October/November 2007 Issue, Volume 33 Number 7, Page 44. After 30 years in practice, this corporate counsel launched a new seafaring life and a new career. In this article she shares what led her to recapture her dream.

Gardner, Howard. *Five Minds for The Future.* Cambridge: Harvard Business School Press, 2006. Building on his earlier works he outlines the five new cognitive abilities that will be essential in our rapidly changing world.

Handy, Charles. *The Age of Paradox.* Cambridge: Harvard Business School Press, 1994. Building on his earlier book, The Age of Unreason, Handy writes about the paradoxes of our time and how we can find meaning and continuity in our lives.

Hillman, James. *Kinds of Power–A Guide to Its Intelligent Uses.* New York: Doubleday, 1995. A most intriguing excursion on real power and how to use it.

Hollis, James. *Finding Meaning in the Second Half of Life: How to Finally, Really Grow Up.* New York: Gotham Books, 2005. Jungian psychoanalyst Hollis believes it is only in the second half of life that we can truly come to know who we are and thus create a life that has meaning. He explores the ways we can grow and evolve to fully become ourselves when the traditional roles of adulthood aren't quite working for us, revealing a new way of uncovering and embracing our authentic selves.

Leider, Richard. *Claiming Your Place at the Fire.* San Francisco: Berrett-Koehler Publishers, 2004. For "people who are ready to stoke the wisdom gained in the first half of their lives to burn with a brighter sense of purpose in the second half," Leider provides a guide to an internal, spiritual search for the purpose of one's older years.

Leider, Richard. *Repacking Your Bags.* San Francisco: Berrett-Koehler Publishers, 2002. As a guide for success in living a more authentically meaningful life, it provides a simple yet elegant process to help people ask the right questions -- and get the right answers -- along the way.

Schuster, John. *Answering Your Call: A Guide for Living Your Deepest Purpose.* San Francisco: Berrett-Koehler Publishers, 2003. Schuster explains what it means to be called to something larger than ourselves -- to find the life that best fits us because it uses our talents to the fullest and adds the most lasting value to the world.

Whyte, David. *The Heart Aroused: Poetry and the Preservation of the Soul in Corporate America.* New York, NY: Doubleday, 1994. A poet's touch to corporate awakenings - original and moving. The Heart Aroused attempts to keep what is tried and true, good and efficient, at the center of our present work life, while opening ourselves to a mature appreciation of the hidden places where our passions and our creativity lie waiting.

LEADERSHIP BOOKS

Bennis, Warren. *On Becoming a Leader.* Reading, MA: Perseus, Revised, 2003. A recently revised classic by a major figure in the leadership realms.

Block, Peter. *Community: The Structure of Belonging.* San Francisco: Berrett-Koehler Publishers, 2008. Block explores a way of thinking about our places that creates an opening for authentic communities to exist, and details what each of us can do to make that happen.

Charan, Ram, Drotter, Stephen, Noel, James. *The Leadership Pipeline.* San Francisco: Jossey Bass, 2001. This book provides a useful framework for understanding the tasks and challenges for leadership development at each consecutive step up the ladder.

Collins, Jim. *From Good To Great.* New York, NY: Harper Collins Publishers, 2001. Author of Built to Last, Collins examines nearly 1500 companies to determine the necessary factors in moving from good to great.

Dotlich, David L., et al. *Leadership Passages: The Personal and Professional Transitions that make or break a leader.* San Francisco: Jossey Bass, 2004. The authors articulate thirteen common personal and professional transitions that can make or break a leader. Much like our Cycle of Renewal they stress the point that transitions are predictable and inevitable.

Drucker, Peter F. *The Essential Drucker.* New York: NY: Collins Publishers, 2003. Management guru and 30 year professor at Claremont College; this compilation serves as a summary of some of his most noteworthy work.

Heifetz, Ronald A. *Leadership without Easy Answers.* Boston, MA: Harvard University Press, 1994. Founding director of JFK's Center for Public Leadership, Heifetz has written extensively on leadership. Written for public and private leaders, the core of his contribution distinguishes between routine technical problems and adaptive problems.

Helgesen, Sally. *The Female Advantage.* New York, NY: Currency Doubleday Press, 1995. An interesting look at the unique advantages women have in the leadership role.

Kanter, Rosabeth Moss. *Confidence: How Winning Streaks & Losing Streaks Begin.* New York, NY: Crown Business Books, 2004. Based on 300 interviews with leaders, Kanter explains the important role of confidence in a leader's performance over time.

Kouzes, James M., Posner, Barry Z. *The Leadership Challenge.* San Francisco: Jossey Bass, 2002. Well-known leadership book highlighting the research these authors did uncovering the key elements necessary for ordinary people to become great leaders.

Sandholtz, Kurt et al. *Beyond Juggling: Rebalancing Your Busy Life.* San Francisco: Berrett-Koehler Publishers, 2002. The authors offer strategies and tools to help you craft a rebalancing plan, tailored to your life needs and career situation.

Sharpnack, Rayona. *Trade Up! – Five Steps for Redesigning Your Leadership and Life from the Inside Out.* San Francisco: Jossey-Bass, 2007. These five steps will help leaders gain awareness of assumptions that may no longer be valid, and free them to trade up from limiting beliefs and behaviors to those that will help them change the world and improve the meaningfulness of their lives.

Silsbee, Doug. *Presence-Based Coaching: Cultivating Self-Generative Leaders Through Mind, Body and Heart.* San Francisco: Jossey Bass, 2008. Silsbee offers a practical map to the territory of working with presence, both within yourself and in your coaching and developing of others.

CAREER DEVELOPMENT BOOKS

Bronson, Po. *What Should I Do with My Life?: The True Story of People Who Answered the Ultimate Question.* New York: Random House, Inc. 2002. The premise, that "nothing is braver than people facing up to their own identity," is explored around issues of self-determination, paradoxes of money and meaning, authorship and destiny, brain candy and novelty versus soul food.

Craddock, Maggie. *The Authentic Career: Following the Path of Self-Discovery to Professional Fulfillment.* Novato, CA: New World Library, 2004. Craddock outlines a four-stage therapeutic process that carefully separates what the reader wants and needs from the often-frustrating demands of family and work, believing that identifying authentic career goals and strategies requires a careful examination of one's inner life.

Dorsey, Jason Ryan. *My Reality Check Bounced! – The Twentysomething's Guide to Cashing In on Your Real-World Dream.* New York: Broadway Books, 2007. Filled with honest stories about young adults who have searched deep inside to find the happiness they were missing, Dorsey provides concrete action steps to live with more passion and purpose.

Ibarra, Herminia. *Working Identity: Unconventional Strategies for Reinventing Your Career.* Boston: Harvard Business School Press, 2003. For those who are feel stuck because they feel they should be doing something completely different but don't know what it is yet, Ibarra illustrates how to make radical transitions one day at a time through the examples of 23 people who have successfully made the plunge from just a career to a whole new lifestyle.

Kaye, Beverly & Jordan-Evans, Sharon. *LOVE IT - Don't Leave It – 26 Ways to Get What You Want at Work.* San Francisco: Berrett-Koehler Publisher, 2003. A book that inspires workers to take charge of their own destinies and shows how to make the most of your work environment.

Leider, Richard, Shapiro, David. *Whistle While You Work.* San Francisco: Berrett-Koehler, 2001. Examines individual's core gifts in an effort to identify what one's work ought to be about.

Melcher, Michael. *The Creative Lawyer: A Practical Guide to Authentic Professional Satisfaction.* American Bar Association: 2007. Attorney Melcher provides a step-by-step method for imagining and realizing your path to personal and professional satisfaction.

Wilner, Abby and Stocker, Catherine. *The Quarterlifer's Companion – How to Get on the Right Career Path, Control Your Finances, and Find the Support Network You Need to Thrive.* New York: McGraw-Hill, 2005. An instructional manual for twenty-somethings in dealing with work issues, money problems, relationships, and life.

LIFECYCLE EMPOWERMENT BOOKS

Adson, Patricia R. *A Princess & Her Garden – A Fable of Awakening & Arrival.* Red Wing, MN: Lone Oak Press, 1999. Written by a psychotherapist, this book presents the story of a woman who learns how to maintain the delicate balance between care of herself and caring for others.

Block, Peter. *The Answer to How is Yes: Acting on What Matters.* San Francisco: Berrett Koehler Press, 2002. Author of well-known

Flawless Consulting, Block focuses here on empowerment, stewardship, accountability and reconciliation.

Borchard, David C. *Will the Real You Please Stand Up?: Find Passion in Your Life and Work.* Pittsburgh, PA: SterlingHouse Publisher, Inc, 2006. Borchard reveals a methodology for for digging up that buried treasure of your being and setting off on a new journey.

Borchard, David C. *The Joy of Retirement – Finding Happiness, Freedom, and the Life You've Always Wanted.* New York: AMACOM, 2008. Borchard shows how to achieve fulfillment and meaning by confronting six major life issues.

Eisenberg, Lee. *The Number – A completely Different Way to Think About the Rest of Your Life.* New York: Free Press, 2006. A provocative guide to our psyches and finances that will help you think about the kind of life you want and the kind of money you need to achieve it.

Hassler, Christine. *20 Something Manifesto: Quarter-Lifers Speak Out About Who They Are, What They Want, and How to Get It.* Novato, CA: New World Library, 2008. Hassler presents one of the biggest problems that twentysomethings face: "Expectation Hangovers," in which reality doesn't measure up to what they had come to expect from their lives, and then addresses three questions that dominate the decade.

Hudson, Frederic M. *The Adult Years: Mastering the Art of Self Renewal.* San Francisco: Jossey-Bass, Revised 2000. A masterful book on change and continuity throughout the adult years. Hudson helps adults understand life transitions across each decade of their lives.

Furlong, Mary. *Turning Silver into Gold: How to Profit in the New Boomer Marketplace.* Upper Saddle River, NJ: FT Press, 2007. Believing that America's 78 million baby boomers will live more active, creative, inventive lives than any generation before them, Furlong reveals breakthrough product and service opportunities to capitalize on this phenomenon.

Jung, Carl. *The Basic Writings of C. G. Jung.* New York: The Modern Library, 1959.

Jung, Carl. *The Undiscovered Self.* Penguin Books, 1957. Jung states the need for individuals to acquire self-knowledge in order cope with dangers posed by mass society.

Kegan, Robert. *In Over Our Heads – The Mental Demands of Modern Life.* Cambridge, MA: Harvard Business School Press, 1994. Kegan asks the right questions about the current predicaments for adult living.

Lifton, Robert Jay. *The Protean Self – Human Resilience in an Age of Fragmentation.* New York, NY: Basic books, 1993. A magnificent treatise on how to thrive in our age of endless flow, written by one of the finest living scholars on adult life.

Lucas, Mary B. *Lunchmeat & Life Lessons – Sharing a Butcher's Wisdom.* KS: MBL Press, 2006. A butcher's daughter shares the wisdom she gained from her father's lessons on how to deal with life's beginnings and endings and all the ups and downs in between.

McLean, Pamela. *Why a ThirdLaunch™?* Santa Barbara, CA: Hudson Press, 2007. Several factors associated with the Baby Boomers, a generation of 80 million people in the U.S., portends the pioneering of a new stage of life - ThirdLaunch™. McLean identifies the conditions requiring a new stage and provides a map for Boomers to take a leap to make a difference while enjoying new possibilities.

Nash, Laura & Stevenson, Howard. *Just Enough: Tools for Creating Success in Your Work and Life.* New York: John Wiley & Sons, 2004. While the authors propose an interesting framework to help us capture our own definition of success, in their view success comes from four components: happiness, achievement, significance, and legacy.

Neugarten, Bernice L. *The Meanings of Age.* Chicago: The University of Chicago Press, 1996. Asserting that the social structures of society are regarded as fundamental in shaping the individual's experience, Neugarten addresses the theme, social structures and human lives in relation to the dramatic change in the age structure of the population.

Robbins, Alexandra and Wilner, Abby. *Quarterlife Crisis: The Unique Challenges of Life in Your Twenties.* New York: Penguin Putnam, 2001. While the book doesn't contain all the answers that people in their twenties are looking for, it does feature helpful stories they can relate to, describing how other people their age are struggling with similar issues, such as trying to balance work, pleasure, family, friends, and romance.

Salazar, Marcos. *The Turbulent Twenties Survival Guide: Figuring Out Who You Are, What You Want, & Where You're Going After College.* Oakland, CA: New Harbinger Publications, 2006. A roadmap to developing the independence and self-reliance to accomplish goals while coping with uncertainty and doubt, and managing today's overwhelming number of choices.

Sheehy, Gail. *Passages: Predictable Crises of Adult Life.* New York: Ballantine Books, 2006. Sheehy discusses mysteries of the life cycle and presents predictable crises of adulthood.

MANAGING GRIEF AND LOSS
ARTICLES AND BOOKS

Bridges, William. *The Way of Transitions: Embracing Life's Most Difficult Moments.* New York, NY: Perseus Books, 2001. An expert on change, Bridges takes us on his personal journey of transformation as he manages the difficult transition of losing his wife to cancer.

McLean, Pamela. *Career and Caregiving: Integrating Two Roles, Two Lives.* National Career Development Association Monogram, Washington DC, 2008.

MALE DEVELOPMENT BOOKS

Hart, Daniel. *Becoming Men: The Development of Aspirations, Values, and Adaptational Styles.* New York: Springer Publishing, 1992. Hart analyzes the results of an intensive twenty-year longitudinal study of men's development, and develops an original framework for understanding the psychological similarities and differences in men's lives.

Levant, Ronald & Pollack, William. *A New Psychology Of Men.* New York: Basic Books, 2003. By synthesizing the latest research, clinical experience, and major theoretical perspectives on men and by figuring in cultural, class, and sexual orientation differences, the authors illuminate the many variations of male behavior.

FEMALE DEVELOPMENT BOOKS

Bartlett, Pam. *Women Connected – A Session-by-Session Coaching Guide for Women's Groups.* Greenbank, WA: Glenmoore Press, 2007. A guide to help you discover your true purpose, reconnect with your passions, and put your dreams into motion. This book contains a rich collection of activities, personal stories and words of wisdom.

Coughlin, Lin, Wingard, Ellen, Hollihan, Keith. *Enlightened Power: How Women are Transforming the Practice of Leadership.* San Francisco: Jossey Bass, 2005.

Hewlett, Sylvia Ann. *Creating a Life: Professional Women and the Quest for Children.* New York, NY: Hyperion Press, 2002.

COUPLES DEVELOPMENT BOOKS

Brody, Steve, Broady, Cathy. *Renew Your Marriage at Midlife.* New York, NY: Putnam, 1998. The authors capture the main themes of couple's renewal in simple language.

Gottman, John M. *The Seven Principles for Making Marriage Work.* New York, NY: Three Rivers Press, 1999. An ultimate guide to marital fitness including an at-home, step-by-step process for renewing one's marriage.

Heiter, Susan M. *From Conflict to Resolution – Skills and Strategies for Individual, Couple and Family Therapy.* New York, NY: Norton, 1990. Great book on relationship realignment.

FAMILY DEVELOPMENT BOOKS

Apter, Terri. *The Myth of Maturity: What Teenagers Need from Parents to Become Adults.* New York, NY: Norton, 2001. Apter offers a different perspective on our latest generation of young adults – highlighting the turbulence of the 1-24 transition time.

SPIRITUAL DEVELOPMENT BOOKS

Chopra, Deepak. *How to Know God: The Soul's Journey into the Mystery of Mysteries.* China: Running Press Book Publishers, 2001. According to Chopra, the brain is hardwired to know God. The human nervous system has seven biological responses that correspond to seven levels of divine experience. Identifying and harnessing their power will allow you to discover the divine within yourself.

Chodron, Pema. *When Things Fall Apart: Heart Advice for Difficult Times.* Boston: Shambala Publications, 1997. Chodron offers useful advice about how Buddhism helps readers to cope with the grim realities of modern life, including fear, despair, rage and the feeling that we are not in control of our lives.

Palmer, Parker, J. *A Hidden Wholeness.* San Francisco: John Wiley & Sons, Inc., 2004. Palmer coins the phrase "soul versus role" to get our attention in this workaholic society of today.

Schuster, John. *Answering Your Call.* San Francisco: Berrett Koehler Press, 2002. Schuster takes a look at the importance of purpose and calling in one's life.

My Wake-up Call – Lessons Learned

By Frederic M Hudson

My life course was shaped indelibly by a powerful event in my childhood that taught me a great deal about LifeLaunching. Although I have shared this story on many occasions, I repeat it here because it vividly represents the message and purpose of this book: *have a vision, get a plan, and stay on course.*

On August 23, 1942, when I was nine years old, I awakened in silent terror. I was unable to move any part of my body except my eyes. My muscles seemed frozen, and my voice was silenced. Although I had gone to bed as a walking, talking, wiggling boy, I woke up the next day paralyzed with polio. Neither my legs nor my arms would respond to my desperate efforts to move, and my neck and jaw were as rigid as rocks. Breathing was panicked and pain was everywhere. In the 1940's polio was a dreaded epidemic of unidentified origin for which there was no means of prevention, and no real medical treatment. Many who contracted it died; others went through life in braces and wheelchairs.

The next this I remember was lying on the back seat of my parents' old automobile as they drove me thirty miles from my home in upstate New York to a hospital in Syracuse. That journey was unbelievably painful. I was sicker than I had ever felt in my life. I felt a helplessness and fear never experienced before. "What will happen to me?" I pondered. "Am I going to die? Will I ever see my family again? It isn't fair..." That day remains vivid in my mind, like a screeching siren I couldn't turn off.

At the hospital, they placed me on a hard bed – with no pillow, in a quarantine ward. I spent my waking moments staring upward at the ceiling – my only option – and feeling totally helpless. The main treatment I received were Sister Kenny" hot packs administered frequently throughout the day and night, so hot that they scorched my body and smelled like wet, burnt wool – a smell branded to my mind.

A wise nurse named Susan spent lots of time with me. Quiet and caring, she visited me frequently and told me many things.

Her main message went like this: "Your future, Frederic, is hidden on the ceiling, and you are the only one that can find it. Look for what you will be doing as you grow up. It's all up there. Will you be a track star, a tennis player, a scientist? Will you be going on trips to faraway places? Will you be going to summer camps and swimming? Will you go to college and become someone special? Will you marry and have a family? Frederic, all you have to do is to study the ceiling. When you see your future, it will start to happen!

That's all she ever talked about – my future. I spent hours and then days and months searching for snapshots of my future in the maze on the dirty ceiling above my immobile body. There were many designs discernible there, with cracks in the plaster and shadows changing throughout the day. Abundant Rorschach's for me to interpret. The first vision I saw had me running and playing and active again. I actually saw myself as a young deer leaping effortlessly through a forest. After a while, I had only to lift up my eyes and I would see myself bouncing along, alive with graceful movements and amazing speed. Then I saw myself having friends, and laughing again, and climbing trees. After a few months of ceiling gazing, I pictured myself going to college and becoming a husband and father someday. I even envisioned myself as a doctor.

My nurse Susan convinced me that if I would keep rehearsing my vision on the ceiling, sooner or later my body would begin to move again and make it all happen. I never doubted her. At the very time when my body was at its all-time low, I trusted her to coach me toward my highest self. Knowing my eyeballs were my only moving part, she brought a projector into my room and flashed stories and pictures on the ceiling for me to consider as I pondered my future. She projected a checkerboard and taught me how to play checkers and chess as she facilitated a learning environment for my future. She would read me books while instructing me to find my life in the patterns overhead. She brought me music to listen to, and the Braille recordings of famous books. Slowly but surely I began to feel the world of sound and sight open up before me.

She obtained my school assignments for the fourth and fifth grades and tutored me without my even knowing I was doing homework. Honoring my wish to become a medical doctor, Susan procured the graduate bulletins of Yale Harvard, and Columbia medical schools. She deciphered undergraduate prerequisites and distilled the learning process into my age group. Before leaving the hospital she had engaged me with advanced mathematics, the French language, philosophy, and English literature. I felt so privileged to be learning so much I imagined that everyone in my class was in a hospital somewhere – with polio – learning from nurses like Susan!

Before contracting polio, I had not been much of a student. My family was struggling to survive the Depression and World War II, and I was squeezed in between a brother a year older and a sister a year younger. Life was a constant scramble, day by day. My father worked in a pharmaceutical manufacturing plant, and my mother worked part-time as a clerk in a drug store.

But during my months in the hospital, in my desperate physical condition, time was all I had, second after second, and I wanted to learn everything I could. I wanted to become everything I could become. And I believed magically that what I envisioned on the ceiling would come to pass. Everything I imagined seemed possible, and what did I have to lose? Except for me, the room was silent and empty. I had no radio and TV had not yet been invented. Thank God! It took great gobs of silence to find my soul and invent my future.

One day, as I was entranced in a forest walk along the cracks in the ceiling, I felt a wiggle in the toes of my left foot. It was not much, but it was *everything*. I could move my toes, a little When Susan made her rounds, she assured me that this was the beginning of my future unfolding – not merely my getting well but my visions being realized. She said my strength would slowly return up my legs, my backbone and arms, and finally my upper neck and chin. "You are now in training," she would so, "so practice moving your foot for the rest of the month." She tied a string to my toes up through an eyelet she screwed into the ceiling (and I winced when she made a hold in the secret garden of my mind's eye), and secured a small bell to it. "Ring the bell,' she insisted, and indeed I did, having no knowledge of Pavlov and his dog.

I was astounded that Susan knew the path to my recovery and transformation. She placed twine around my foot, up through a pulley (screwed into the ceiling!) and down to a handle on a casement window to my right. "Frederic," she whispered, "make the window go open and closed until it makes so much noise that every nurse on the floor scolds you." High motivation for a nine-year old, and although I was unable to move my foot for weeks or months, my attention was completely riveted to doing so. In time, it happened, and only years later did I learn that all the nurses were instructed by Susan to rush into my room to complain royally. In time, my room looked like a gymnasium, with ropes going in various directions to engage my awakening limbs with necessary exercise. I loved my room, and I had no intention of ever leaving. As ugly and bereft as it was, it was my secret garden. Never before had I been so awake, alive, and ready to soar. The last things to cooperate were my neck and upper chest, I have been eternally grateful for everything I learned and became in my recovery. I now walk, run, play tennis, and live without any noticeable deficit.

The hardest thing I ever did was to leave that room. I cried in anguish as my wheelchair left the hospital for my uncle's farm, where I was quarantined to learn to walk again. My loneliness there was punctuated by the deadly; daily visits of an orthopedic nurse who made me exercise, without any of the mentoring Susan commanded. It was months before I could walk, but when I did, I reentered my family system and schooling as someone with a vision of where I was going and how I would get there. I had a purpose and I planned my life around it. Susan's voice continued for years as a refrain in my head: vision, plan, train, and become the best that you can be.

I did not fully grasp what Susan had taught me until midlife, when I was struggling mightily with my path and life course. By then I had shifted from becoming a doctor of medicine to becoming a doctor of philosophy. After earning a Ph.D. at Columbia University – one of the schools recommended by Susan – I became a professor of philosophy at Colby College in Maine, and then at the University of San Francisco. I also became a husband and father. I wrote some books, became a good public speaker, and 'arrived' at the goals I had conjured up with Susan.

In my late thirties, when my youth felt spent, I thought my life was over. I was out of vision. After much soul-searching, I returned to what I had learned from Susan – to be visionary and responsible for my own future. Since I remained close friends with Susan until her death in 1989, I phoned to get her advice, and this is what she blurted out: "yesterday's dreams are not always tomorrow's promises, Frederic. Gaze at the sky above you as if you were in the hospital again, and get a new fix on where you are going, and why. What we need at midlife is not always what we wanted when we were young. But find the fire, the passion, and the hope that belongs to you. It's always up there, ready to be loaned to the right person at the right time." I cried with joy.

So again, I learned painfully, to gaze at the ceiling of my life to find new paths into my future. I am telling my story so every reader can benefit from Susan's simple wisdom:

- See how you want your life to unfold.

- Look for your best choices.

- Trust your vision.

- Create a detailed plan to get from her to there.

- Take full responsibility for your life course: time manage every detail.

- Find the best resources available for empowering your future. Network, train, travel, seek, adventure.

- Learn how to learn, unlearn, and relearn. Make learning your central business.

- Live on the outer edge of your possible reaches, not on the inner edge of your security.

Thank you, Susan!

Index